50 Ways to Love Your Community

Sarah Cline, Ph.D.

Contents

Introduction

In *50 Ways to Love Your Community*, we embark on an exploration beyond the familiar boundaries of our daily lives, challenging the notion of community as a mere backdrop to individual existence. This volume of the 50 Ways series offers a foray into the many ways we can engage with, contribute to, and ultimately enrich the communities we inhabit.

Too often, we find ourselves ensconced within our personal bubbles, navigating the same routes, interacting with a fixed circle of acquaintances, and adhering to established routines. Such insularity, while comfortable, can blind us to the vibrant people, ideas, and opportunities that surround us. This book aims to puncture these bubbles, inviting readers to look beyond the familiar and engage with others in meaningful, exciting ways.

The concept of community extends far beyond geographical boundaries or shared interests. It encompasses the intricate web of connections, shared responsibilities, and collective aspirations that bind us together.

Together, we'll cover a diverse range of subjects, each highlighting a different facet of engagement. From the power of local economies and the importance of public spaces to the role of art in communal identity and the impact of individual actions on collective well-being, this book provides a comprehensive overview of what it means to truly love and contribute to one's greater home—big or small.

Each chapter is designed to inspire action, providing practical strategies that readers can adopt to make a tangible difference. Whether it's through volunteering, participating in local governance, supporting local businesses, or simply fostering a deeper sense of connection with those around us, the book offers a variety of pathways to an enriched existence.

Are you ready to look at your community differently, moving beyond your usual routine and seeing what's really happening around you? Interested in joining a local project, helping out at local events, or simply getting to know your neighbors better? If you're up for these practical steps to make a positive impact where you live, this book is for you. Let's get started, and you soon may find a whole new world right down the street!

Chapter 1

Group Gains and True Selfhood

In the intricate design of human existence, there is an incredible desire for connection and belonging. In fact, it is fundamental. From tribes in ancient civilizations to the most modern of social networks, humans have always sought the comfort and support found within groups. Beyond the surface-level camaraderie, there exists a deeper, more profound psychological benefit to belonging—a benefit that truly enhances individual well-being.

Belonging to a group offers various psychological advantages. First of all, it provides a sense of identity and purpose, both of which foster feelings of acceptance, validation, and security. With a supportive community, individuals can find solace in knowing they are not alone, especially in their struggles. This sense of unity can really help to bolster your mental health by reducing stress and anxiety while promoting overall happiness and fulfillment.

Having a sense of belonging is so important, especially considering the groups and labels we give ourselves and those around us. All of us are members of families, teams, clubs, and spiritual groups/churches. We also are involved in charities, and political parties, and reside in cities, countries, and even have our own nationalities to consider. Nearly every aspect of our lives is organized around belonging to something—some sort of group or collective.

The sense of belonging is critical to the way humanity organizes itself. If social interaction and belonging weren't important, we would live solitary lives, only coming together to procreate (to maintain the species) and then quickly kick the children out of our homes and lives as soon as they could walk. We wouldn't have families, communities, or even organized government.

A sense of belonging is ingrained in us—it's in the very foundation of who we are as a species. And we can't even separate the importance of it from our physical or mental health as it has an effect on both.

The social ties that accompany the feeling of belonging help manage stress and behavioral issues. When we feel we have support and are not alone, we are often more resilient, having the ability to cope more effectively. Coping well with hardships aids in both physical and mental well-being and is a direct result of having positive social ties. This ability is usually introduced early in life. In fact, we begin life with the most crucial of needs—attachment to a caregiver. This is the beginning of the fundamental need we have for belonging. Studies have shown that children who have not had the opportunity to achieve a healthy attachment have lower self-esteem, a more negative outlook, are not able to trust, and can have an overall perception of being rejected.

Depression, anxiety, andsuicide are common mental health conditions associated with lacking a sense of belonging. These conditions can lead to social behaviors that interfere with one's ability to connect to others in any real or meaningful way, which can create a cycle of events that make it even more difficult to achieve a sense of belonging.

So, what can you do to increase the sense of belonging in your community and yourself?

- **Make an effort:** The most crucial ingredient to building a sense of belonging is effort. You cannot belong if you don't choose to make the effort to engage with others and help others feel like they also belong. It may feel uncomfortable at first to meet new people, but with time, it can become easier. Due to this difficulty, it may be worth considering the fact that you may need to practice self-talk. The more you practice self-talk, breathe positivity, and make an effort to engage, the actions will become like second nature.

- **Be mindful of others:** While it's important to love yourself and put yourself first at times, it's equally important to be conscious of others. By thinking less about yourself while with others and making sure the other person or group is where your focus lies, the more compassionate you will seem to others—and the stronger your relationships can become. Making conversation with others and helping them feel heard is critical to increasing your sense of belonging. It is important to mutually ask questions, make small talk, self-disclose skillfully, and truly listen to people's responses in order to form a proper relationship.

- **Keep and teach an open mind:** Try new activities and meet new people. Consider new ways of thinking. Lead by example so others who may look up to you can see how it works. Put in effort to seek activities and groups of people whom you have things in common with.

- **Practice an attitude of acceptance:** Recognize that

others have different ways of being which don't have to change you and you don't necessarily have to agree with. Focus on the similarities rather than the differences. Similarities tend to increase bonding—as does positivity. If you feel that people are not like you, that doesn't mean that they won't make great friends down the road. Focus on a mutual goal, such as a volunteer opportunity or hobby you may have in common to find a good grappling hook to anchor your relationship.

- **Validate action:** Think about it: if creating a sense of belonging for others is challenging for you, it is likely challenging for others too. Give everyone in your community the encouragement you might give yourself—and the benefit of the doubt. Validate them, just like you need to validate your own actions and work together to build friendships and grow your community into something worthy of love.

Key Takeaways:

Chapter 1 of *50 Ways to Love Your Community* has considered the importance of belonging. Belonging to a community (or social group in general) provides a sense of identity and purpose, which in turn leads to feelings of acceptance, validation, and security. Through supportive relationships, individuals find solace in knowing they are not alone in their struggles, which promotes mental well-being and reduces stress and anxiety.

Chapter 2

Communicate with Your Community

Effective communication is the foundation of any healthy relationship, and therefore a main cornerstone in maintaining a happy and healthy life. Human beings are social creatures, and no matter how introverted you may be, you still need others in your life to be happy and productive. Regardless of the relationship, communication is necessary. It is the bridge that connects us all, enables us to come to mutual understandings, and builds stronger bonds between us.

In this chapter, we'll delve into the essential components of communication that can strengthen the bond you have with others.

While it's easy to be swayed by the idea that love is a mysterious force beyond our control, the reality is that developing and maintaining lasting relationships require a lot more than just love and acceptance. It requires conscious effort, respect, and a willingness to understand one another on a deeper level. This journey of appreciation goes beyond knowing people's favorite "things" or doing what you think will make them "happy". It's about diving deep into their psyche (and yours), comprehending their unique personality traits (and yours), and recognizing how other people's attributes interact with yours in a way that can formulate a healthy and lasting relationship—all of which can, in turn, create a positive community.

In the age of digital connections and instant gratification, we sometimes forget the beauty of human interaction. We often overlook the importance of patience, reflection, and presence with others. At times, we also let external factors beyond that pull us away from what truly matters. By fostering an environment of open communication and mutual respect, you're not just building relationships and bonds but cultivating relationships that thrive on understanding, compassion, and genuine connection with your neighbors. Using this guide, you can learn strategies and ground rules to help you convey your emotions effectively.

Understand and Practice Active Listening with Neighbors

Communicating is fundamentally a shared process between two or more people. It's a two-way street. You are never going to be the only one talking, which also means it will eventually be your turn to listen as well. Think about how much you want to feel heard when you speak to others. The other person likely wants to feel heard just as much. Although it may feel counterintuitive, don't start with talking in your conversations. Start with listening. This is because listening is validating to the other person. And if you *are* a talker—don't worry! Your turn will come.

It's also important to acknowledge that being skilled at listening means being aware that there may be more under the surface—more than what's being said. Instead of making assumptions about what you see or hear, understand that it is important that you have clarity. The full scope of proper listening should include:

- **Giving your undivided attention:** Put the phone down

and minimize other distractions or interruptions. If you are stressed or anxious then regulate breathing to relax. You can't focus on them if your mind is swirling with anxieties. Be prepared to reorient your attention back to the person you're listening to if your thoughts waver.

- **Being supportive:** When someone is speaking and it's clear that they need support—offer it to them! Use your words and your body language to show that you are engaged. This encourages them to continue and shows them that you're truly listening to what they have to say.

- **Being empathic:** Empathy means to understand someone else's situation from their point of view. It's okay to disagree with someone but learn to let go of preconceived ideas and wait while they explain their perspective so you can understand where they're coming from. You can better state your position once you understand theirs. Do not interrupt or finish sentences.

- **Being patient:** Let them set the pace of the conversation. Don't interrupt them or finish their sentences and never speak in a way that makes them feel like they need to rush.

- **Going beyond words:** Sometimes nonverbal cues, such as the body language of the other person, provide information. Look for facial expressions, body gestures, and eye movements for more detail about what they're saying.

- **Finding the big picture:** Remember that the person speaking is communicating their ideas with you. Take all the information provided to you (verbally and nonverbally) and ask follow-up questions as necessary. Make sure that you understand the big picture.

Express Your Emotions with Yourself and Others

Everyone has emotions. It's natural. Expressing them, however, isn't something that's always easy. Getting in touch with your feelings can not only help you understand others—it can help others understand you better, too.

In fact, being understood and accepted are universal needs that we have—we, as humans, crave that kind of connection. So, when you share your experiences and emotions with others, you're more likely to connect in deep and meaningful ways with them. You're also more likely to get your needs met, which in turn leads to happier and healthier relationships overall.

Sharing your feelings *can* be a daunting proposition. When you share your feelings, you allow yourself to be vulnerable. This vulnerability can be scary; after all, it leaves you open to the possibility of being hurt, but it can also lead to the deepest connections.

Understand Your Own Feelings

Before you can express your feelings, you, yourself, have to know what they are. For most people, it helps to have some quiet time to reflect, especially if you aren't naturally intuitive to feelings or emotions. Try taking ten minutes per day for the sole purpose of contemplating how you feel about your life at the present time. Try to identify your feelings, remembering that you can have more than one feeling at once. Explore what's been happening in your life that may be related to your feelings.

Be Selective with Who You Share With

Your feelings are intimate parts of yourself; they shouldn't be shared with just *anyone*. The truth of the matter is that there are times when it's appropriate to be vulnerable with others, and times it isn't. Additionally, there are also times when you are not meant to forge a deep connection with certain people. Make sure that you proceed slowly and begin by sharing feelings that feel safer and less vulnerable before diving in head-first, especially if you aren't the type to generally share intimate details. If those small vulnerabilities are received well, share a little bit more and go from there.

Respond—Don't React!

Sometimes we make the mistake of trying to communicate our feelings in a moment of heightened emotion when we aren't regulated. This tends to result in blurting things out before we have processed them or even so much as had the chance to calm down—which leads to miscommunication, stating untruth, and/or pointing fingers. Take the time, regulate, and come back to the conversation. It is perfectly acceptable to ask to take a break from a heated conversation or wait until you have had time to calm down and prepare what you need to discuss.

Make Sure the Time Is Right

Be intentional about when you try to communicate your feelings, too! Think about who you are trying to communicate with and their schedule. Oftentimes, people try to communicate their needs at the wrong times. You never want it to be while the other person is distracted, busy, under the influence, sleepy, or even just in a poor mood. Sometimes this means planning ahead and asking for time to be set aside.

In general, make sure that you also try to communicate face-to-face. Technology is convenient, but remember that sometimes context is lost in the written word—and besides, it's less personal and vulnerable. The entire point is to deepen the connection.

Be Direct

Understand that effective communication is clear and direct. It's easier to be direct when you know what you're going to say. Plan your conversation—or at least talking points.

Pay Attention to Body Language and Tone

We have discussed a bit of body language in the previous sections. When communicating, body language is just as important as what you're verbally saying and so is the tone in which you are speaking. Sometimes it's difficult to gauge the tone of your own voice. Sometimes we raise our voices without realizing it, or close ourselves off with our facial expressions and body language—even if we want to communicate appropriately. Be aware of how you're coming across to others when communicating.

Have Emotional Check-Ins with Yourself and Others

Emotional check-ins are an important aspect of life. They are not only important so that you can check in with your friends and family and how they feel your relationship is going/or how they are doing in their everyday lives—but emotional check-ins are also good to participate in with yourself.

We live so much of our day outside of ourselves and it quickly becomes second nature to forget to pull yourself back in and check in with yourself. We engage in conversations with others at work, at home, and even on social media. We read stories, news articles, and the opinions of others almost constantly. And in our downtime, we try to give a little energy to those close to us. It seems our mental space is almost always occupied. But it's important to open up a bit of internal conversation for your own sanity.

Spending time with yourself can sometimes even feel like another task on your miles-long to-do list, but it truly is an essential part of taking care of your emotional wellness and mental health. Just as you would exercise your physical body, "working out" your mind will help keep you balanced even with the stress of day-to-day life.

Checking in with yourself means carving out time every day to ask yourself how you're doing—in life in general, in your relationships, in your job, etc. In this space, you are afforded an opportunity to sort out your emotions, assess your physical and emotional needs, and make an intentional plan on how to address these needs moving forward.

Self-Reflection Time

Choose a time of day when you're the least likely to be interrupted, turn on your favorite tunes, and have a good thinking session. People often complete self-reflection through specific tasks. Two main ones are:

- **Journaling:** If you express yourself best through the written word (looking at you, list-makers), grab your notebook and set aside a quick daily writing session. Even one minute is better than none.

- **Meditation:** Mindfulness is all about becoming aware of your emotions and watching them pass with non-judgment. The meditation seat is an excellent place to work on the skill of checking in and letting go.

Start simple when you check in with others. Send a text or make a phone call. The act doesn't have to be grand or time-consuming. However, if you would like something a little more intimate, ask them out for coffee or lunch. Whichever format you choose, it's important to follow some key principles:

- **Prepare to be vulnerable**: Sharing with your friend is an incredibly powerful experience and is truly beneficial to the relationship, but it can also be a little more difficult to be vulnerable with a friend or other family member than with your partner. Be prepared to be vulnerable if necessary.

- **Be confidential:** Remember that trust is critical in any relationship. No one tells you something in confidence that they want you to spread around. Make sure that you're willing to keep the conversation between you and your friend if you're going to let them tell you anything of merit.

- **Know that you don't have to fix the issue:** No one is expecting you to wave a magic wand and fix everything that is going wrong in your friend's life. Most of the time, your loved one doesn't even want you to. Often, they just want a friendly shoulder to lean on and a pair of listening ears.

Make sure that if you haven't seen each other in a while, whether it's defined as a regular emotional check-in or not, you meet somewhere private so as to not be distracted or disturbed.

Learn What it Means to Be Compassionate

Sharing feelings is a part of all relationships. In all healthy relationships, it's important to care about each other's feelings and strive to meet each other's needs. It all needs to be reciprocal. In order to do all of this, you must tap into your compassion.

Compassion and empathy are different yet closely related. Empathy is our feeling of awareness and our attempt at putting ourselves in another's shoes. Compassion is an emotional response to that empathy and having a desire to help. Empathy is simply understanding the shared humanity that we have with another person, whereas compassion adds another dimension.

Communicate to Understand—Not to Respond

One of the biggest hurdles that people face when it comes to arguments is their communication styles. More specifically, if one or both parties lack proper listening skills. Often, you may hear someone's words but still have no clue what they really mean. Being a good listener means going beyond that, as we just discussed. Think about it—if you are not really listening, then most of the conversations you're having are one-sided, meaning there is more opportunity to lose what someone else's intentions are. This creates conflict based around miscommunication because you're really having your own conversation if you stop listening to the other person or begin implanting your own ideas into the conversation.

So, how do you know if you need to improve your listening skills? Some of the biggest indicators are the following:

- You get frustrated that someone is taking "too long" to speak.

- Your loved one says "You don't get it" often.

- Your loved one says "You aren't listening" or "That's not what I said".

All of these can indicate deeper problems with listening. And in order to build a stronger connection with your community, you have to know how to listen to others. Another thing to look out for is your own self-interest. It's human nature. When something is interesting, we are more apt to listen versus when we are bored. When you're bored, your listening skills quickly deteriorate and that is completely normal. However, if you want to improve your relationships, you must try to shift gears when it comes to your listening skills.

- **Suspend our own agenda:** Stop focusing on what you're going to say while others are talking. You can't listen if you're worried about how to respond.

- **Be interested:** This may be easier said than done. However, if you care for the person speaking, you should have somewhat of an interest in how they're feeling about a particular situation. Focus on their feelings.

- **Be a reporter:** Sometimes when you're communicating and you are trying to boost your listening skills, it helps to pretend you're a reporter and you have to know enough to write about the conversation. Take mental notes (or physical ones if it's appropriate to do so).

- **Ask questions:** This also helps engage your loved one when they're speaking. When you follow up with questions, you're not only gaining clarity for something you may not understand, but you're also showing that you are listening, are invested in the conversation, and understand where they're coming from.

- **Make eye contact and use minimal encouragers:** This also helps with not being distracted. If you're looking at their eyes, you're not looking at your phone, or other people or things that may distract you from the conversation. Just as you're reading their body language, they're reading yours. Use verbal encouragement to show them that not only are you undistracted and looking at them, but that you're also encouraging them to continue with what it is that they are saying.

- **Avoid judgment:** Whether you agree or not does not matter. Focus on understanding their perspective and aim to find out why they feel the way they do without imparting judgment—besides, you don't know what their message is completely if you interrupt them. Interrupting is a waste of time. It not only can frustrate your loved one, but it can make you lose the trajectory of the information.

- **Don't give unsolicited advice:** One of the biggest takeaways you can have when looking to improve your listening skills is that when someone is speaking to you about something important, they always want you to fix it or give your advice. Sometimes people just want to vent or communicate their stance. If they ask for your advice, give it—if not, don't give advice. Just be there.

- **Avoid defensiveness:** Focus on their perspective for the time being. Not yours. Once they finish, you can take the appropriate time needed to respond, especially if you have somehow felt attacked by what they've said.

- **Take responsibility:** Act on what has been said. If your loved one has communicated with you something about yourself—even if it's been difficult to hear—take some responsibility for it. You may need to defend yourself but take the proper time to reflect to know if the defense is warranted or not. Sometimes an apology is necessary instead. Sometimes, though, you will need to defend yourself or explain yourself if you feel you're being judged too harshly. Just make sure the proper care is taken. However, if after the conversation you realize that you do need to make changes, make sure you do so. Meaningful conversation will lose its power if loved ones cannot trust you to apply what has been shared.

- **Follow up with questions:** Our personal feelings, assumptions, judgments, and/or beliefs can often distort what we hear someone saying. As the listener, your role is to understand what is truly being said. This may require you to reflect and ask appropriate questions or re-tell what they just told you to ensure you understood. Summarize what you heard.

Forgive and Make Peace

Do you ever find yourself stuck in a cycle of dwelling on past events or maybe even traumas, replaying conversations long over with, or even regretting decisions you previously made? It's a common struggle, feeling like you're trapped in a time loop where the past holds more power over you than the present does. Breaking free from this pattern is not only possible but it is necessary for personal growth and happiness.

Forgiveness does not mean that you have to entertain having toxic people in your life, or even saying that whatever happened in the past was okay. It's merely letting go of the negativity surrounding the situation for your benefit.

In fact, if there is trauma there, and steps haven't been made to form a healthy, flourishing relationship, you shouldn't even entertain keeping a neighbor or community member in your life. You shouldn't put up with it from any friend or family member. A community member or neighbor is no exception.

However, breaking free from the past is essential as long as you understand that it is not ignoring or denying what has happened; it's merely about accepting it and moving forward with purpose and resilience. You will feel free and have a wonderful opportunity to flourish and enjoy your community for what it is if you're able to do so.

Communicate Boundaries

Knowing how to set boundaries is one of the most essential yet overlooked social skills there is. For some reason, as human beings, we feel guilty for setting boundaries. We make it seem more rooted in selfishness than love; but in reality, boundaries are necessary in all relationships and must be communicated.

Set Appropriate Boundaries and Change Them as Relationships Evolve

Boundaries are "fences" or "lines" that are critical. Setting boundaries is an act that paves the way for understanding and respect. Our friends, family, neighbors, and colleagues often help us figure out who we are, and they're there for us when things are difficult. They also share our joys and successes. However, there are also times when your relationship dynamics change, or when each of you evolves, whether together or independently of one another. Boundaries need to be re-established as things change.

Learn to Say No

If you're a "yes" person, that's great. However, learning how to say "no" is a critical first step in setting boundaries. Saying "yes" continually in any relationship is a great way to feel overwhelmed, which can lead to burnout. This can be detrimental to your relationships as you can start to resent your loved ones in the future. Don't do things that make you uncomfortable or that you just don't feel you want to do. You don't have to say "no" all the time, especially if you're a people-pleaser, but consider mixing it in from time to time, especially when necessary to your mental or physical health. Remember, a true loved one will leave space for you to give yourself a little self-care. A "no" will never compromise a healthy relationship.

Redirect

Difficult conversations have to happen sometimes. Boundary setting can be a particularly challenging conversation, so much so that you often don't want to do it more than once if you can help it. Communicating your boundaries effectively the first time can curb the need to redirect. But sometimes, it may be necessary. For instance, if you have set a boundary in which you would prefer one person you know not to complain about someone else the two of you know and they do anyway, try to redirect the conversation. Instead of yelling at them for crossing your boundary, attempt to redirect them. Simply saying something like "I'm sorry everything is difficult between the two of you, but let's talk about something else." This can typically give them enough insight to understand that you're not interested in continuing the conversation. If they press further, stand your ground and be even more stern.

Don't Be Afraid to Ask for What You Need

No matter how you spin it, people are not mind readers. No matter how much you feel someone knows you, they won't know exactly what you need unless you ask for it. A really useful skill in life is finding ways to state a need in a respectful way. In fact, this is a tool that will benefit you across all relationships, including acquaintanceships, friendships, romantic relationships, and even your professional ones. Letting people know what you need (such as solidarity or space) allows people the chance to respect that request. Without your communication, they might not have the ability to realize what you need and could overwhelm you without meaning to. By communicating your need for solidarity/space, you can successfully avoid conflict or hard feelings.

Validate and Reaffirm

When you first have a "boundary" discussion with someone, it can be truly difficult. It's easy to worry that someone will be hurt, but it's important to understand that there are ways to improve everyone's experience during this conversation. By practicing open dialogue with them, you will be able to develop a sense of how to express yourself to them positively. Reaffirm them and what it is that they do right and/or what you enjoy about them. Affirmations can really reinforce that trust and that in turn makes the conversation a lot more palatable.

Be Direct

Some people may have difficulty with this at first, but it truly is the best policy. Skirting around the subject can often lead to misunderstandings and confusion. Clarity really helps others understand where you are and what you need. They need to understand where they stand with you. Not knowing where people stand with one another can be difficult and cause upset. Your loved ones are likely to be more perceptive in hearing something from you in a direct manner, rather than upsetting you later and not knowing why. So, be direct when asking for what you need! You can be kind and respectful and still be clear as glass!

Respect Differences

When you set boundaries, it's important to note that there will be differences in opinion—and other people may have different boundaries from you, even on the same subject matter. You may have one boundary for yourself for someone to abide by, and they may request something completely different from you. While it's normal to wish that others are different than they are, it is not okay to disrespect their perspective. Issues arise when people become self-righteous, angry, or condescending, especially when dealing with personal boundaries. That is when a situation becomes toxic and potentially abusive.

Diversity can be an absolutely wonderful thing as it makes the world a much more interesting place. Respect your differences, even if those differences can sometimes butt against yours and become frustrating.

Be Consistent

Consistency in your boundaries keeps your expectations clear and focused. It is critical that once you've communicated your boundaries you remain steadfast in upholding them. Consistency involves honoring your limits regardless of circumstances or external pressures. Don't let someone make you feel guilty for your boundaries. In fact, boundaries are an essential part of a relationship and end up creating a healthy atmosphere for care and respect to prosper. It's crucial to stand by your decisions to maintain respect for your own needs. This fosters a mutually respectful relationship.

It is important that you consistently reinforce your boundaries when necessary. If someone unknowingly crosses a boundary, gently remind them. Clear and respectful communication reaffirms the importance of these boundaries and helps maintain understanding.

Set Consequences (If Needed)

In situations where boundaries are repeatedly ignored or violated, establish consequences. This doesn't mean immediately ending the relationship, but it might involve reducing interaction or taking a break to reassess the dynamics you have with another person. Be communicative if this process ends up needing to happen with one of your neighbors/friends.

Prioritize Self-Care

By being consistent in your boundaries, you're also practicing self-care. By focusing on your well-being and not compromising your mental, emotional, or physical health for the sake of avoiding conflict or maintaining a relationship that doesn't respect your limits, you are giving yourself proper care and love. This will only make you better for others, too.

Show Them How to Behave

If boundaries are new with this person, make sure that your behavior aligns with the boundaries you have set for them. You have to show yourself—and them—the same level of respect. For example, if the boundary is about respecting your time, make sure that you respect your own time by not allowing it to be infringed upon. If they're late to a party, start without them. Likewise, model that behavior by respecting their time. Don't be late for their plans if you're asking them not to be late for yours.

Seek Support (if necessary)

If maintaining boundaries becomes challenging or overwhelming, seek support from trusted individuals, such as other friends, a therapist, or a support group. They can provide guidance and encouragement. If you're seeking out support from a non-professional, make sure that you're not gossiping about the situation. This can lead to hurt feelings and a lot more conflict than has already transpired.

Reflect and Adjust When Needed

Periodically reflect on your boundaries and their effectiveness. Assess whether they're serving their purpose. Are you happy? Is everyone else? If necessary, make adjustments to your boundaries based on evolving circumstances or changes in your needs. Make sure that you're asking for others' input as well.

Celebrate Progress

Acknowledge and celebrate your consistency in upholding boundaries as well as others respecting them. Recognize the positive impact it has on your well-being and the health of your relationships moving forward. Celebrating small victories encourages continued commitment from all parties in a relationship.

Maintain Open Communication

Consistency doesn't mean rigidity. Be open to discussing your boundaries if circumstances change or if there's a need for adjustment. Maintaining open lines of communication allows for a better understanding between people. As stated earlier, ask for feedback and make sure that you and your loved one are communicating evenly so that you can both work, mutually, on your relationship.

Practice Patience

Consistency in boundary setting takes time and effort. It can be incredibly draining because it is a continuous process. However, although it is rigorous and might face challenges, it's worth it in the end if everyone is happier as a result. Be patient with yourself and with others as you navigate these boundaries together.

Know and Communicate Your Limits

The ability to recognize your pain or distress requires that you embrace your limits. This goes along with self-care, expressing yourself, reflecting on yourself, finding out what makes you "tick", and setting appropriate boundaries. It all builds on one another. Each of us has inherent limits, including personal limits that are rooted in our own personalities.

For example, one obvious limit is that everyone needs sleep on a regular and consistent basis. However, there are less obvious ones such as "play time". We have all heard the saying "Work hard, play hard", and this is true. We work hard every day—and we do need to play hard, too. This "play" is the time of leisure that every person needs a bit of to maintain their mental health. We need to spend time doing things that bring us joy to prevent burnout and depression. The amount of "play time" depends on the person. Know your limits with this. Your mental health will thank you.

Other examples may include the amount of money you need in your savings account in order to feel prepared for emergencies, as well as your tolerance for certain things (outspoken and angry people, the patience you have for slow drivers, screaming babies, etc.—it's all fair game).

However, although we all have our limits, some people have a difficult time accepting them. There is almost a desire to have no limits, which stems from confusing them with weakness. However, if you recognize that everyone has limits, and find your own, you can more easily notice when you have pushed beyond them. This allows for validation of our own emotions, and therefore the opportunity to learn to regulate by taking a step back from whatever is overstimulating us and refocusing on what it is that we need to do. For example, if you have a highly demanding position at work and have loads and loads of paperwork to finish, and never take a break, it is completely valid to be exhausted and frustrated. By understanding your own emotional distress, you are able to be more compassionate so that you can notice when others have reached their limits as well.

Pinpoint Your Passions (And Show Them Off)

Journeying through life is all about exploration. Discovering and trying new things is a chance to find new passions. This can also be an effective way to grow relationships, too! After all, the key to keeping a strong connection with others is to continually grow alongside them. What better way to bring forth some freshness than to find a fun new hobby you can partake in with people you care for? Or better yet, share some joys you already have with others who may not be familiar with your passions.

When exploring new activities to try in order to pinpoint your passions, consider your interests and preferences as well as the interests and preferences of others (if you're hoping to involve them). You can take turns choosing activities with them ensuring that you each have a say. Be open to trying things you may not have considered before—you might come to find that you enjoy something you never thought you could.

Whether it's trying a new cuisine, taking up a dance class, embarking on a road trip, or learning a new skill, the key is to approach these experiences with an open heart and mind and be willing to embrace the unknown. Know that at the end of the day, even if you don't enjoy the activity, you're doing something different that is sure to create memories and strengthen who you are as well as the relationship with the person you may be experiencing these things with, just by spending quality time together.

Keep in mind that everyone may enjoy different activities. But it's important for you to try things even if you don't think you would enjoy them. You might surprise yourself and find something you are incredibly passionate about. And better yet, you can find common ground with others who may be just as passionate about them!

Travel Somewhere New

Plan and take trips! By yourself, with a friend, with a partner—it doesn't matter; just go! This will help you find even more passions that you didn't even know you had. It can also help develop your own community by implementing customs others might already have in place elsewhere. Broaden your horizon. Just because you're looking to grow your community and learn more ways to love it, doesn't mean you shouldn't look outside of it for inspiration.

Make sure you're exploring new places, cultures, and cuisines since this is what life is all about! In fact, human beings have traveled for centuries. Exploration is almost ingrained in us thickly like an instinct. Historically, travel started out as a purely practical instinct. We traveled for food, better environments, etc. As civilization began to grow, it was mostly done for the purpose of profit and power. Merchants sailed on long journeys to sell their wares and exchange their items for goods needed back home. We exchanged cultures and knowledge throughout different parts of the world with others, and, eventually, we got to where we are now—traveling for fun. Traveling is far easier these days, whether it's in a car, a boat, a plane, a helicopter, a train—it doesn't matter. You can go almost anywhere your heart desires.

Make it Fun

For most people, implementing communication strategies and techniques is something usually thought about when facing a conflict (e.g. marital issues, asking a boss for a raise, addressing children's misbehavior, etc.). However, communication is not just for conflict resolution. In fact, it affects every part of our lives. The good news is that you can also implement a bit of *fun* into your communication strategies in order to create more effective communication with those you choose to interact with, including your community and neighbors.

The Power of Play

Researchers have found that play is essential for developing children. It helps their peace of mind, enables them to learn, teaches them critical social skills, and is even used in therapeutic settings in order to help children assess and express their emotions. Play supports the safe, stable, and nurturing relationships with caregivers that all children need in order to thrive and live healthy lives.

However, play is not just for children. In fact, studies show that adults who incorporate more play in their lives find that they are more productive at work, engage in more positive communication with their loved ones, and overall live more enjoyable and happy lives.

Playing together with others, which is what this guide is all about—our social needs as humans and building a better community—means simply sharing your joy. This is especially true in regard to communication; play can allow you to become more in tune with those around you and even decrease your body's stress response.

Sometimes, the unstructured, spontaneous play that children naturally engage in is difficult for adults—as they typically no longer have the same interests or energy styles as children. However, the power of play can also be harnessed through structured games (card games, video games, board games, etc.) to help adults feel connected to one another and enhance communication. Adding a game night to your weekly routine can be a great way to harness the power of play, and inviting members of the community or neighbors means improving your connections with them!

Some games can improve communication directly by engaging with our language skills. These range from games like Scattergories and Balderdash to more simple games like Uno or Go Fish.

Some games develop other skills like problem-solving, taking turns, reading body language, and negotiating. Most games require communication and even rely heavily on it. Those games include Charades, Clue, Monopoly, and Apples to Apples.

Bare Your Soul via Art

Communication can come in all forms and is not exclusive to verbal exchanges. If we trace the etymology of the word "emotion" back to its Latin roots, we can see that "e" means "out", and "movere" means "to move". In an ideal scenario, emotions flow naturally, but often they can become trapped, whether that's due to past traumas or just from simply not knowing how to express them. No matter the case, it can eventually lead to a buildup of feelings. Our emotions and our experiences can often feel like big burdens to carry. Expressing emotions through art provides a powerful outlet to release these pent-up feelings before they manifest into deeper issues.

Expressing yourself through art goes beyond just stating your feelings on one thing or the next—it's about allowing emotions to flow freely, accepting them, and giving them a voice to communicate with. This process can invigorate you, allowing creativity to spark and flourish.

Engaging in artistic expression is accessible to everyone, and it doesn't matter the talent or skill level. Whether that art is drawing, painting, sculpting, music, movement, writing, or drama, the creative process is accessible and can allow you to open up and reveal your innermost self.

By trying new forms of expression, you can truly uncover talents and aspects of yourself that may have been hidden or unrealized. There are several artistic forms of expression, including:

- **Traditional art**: Whether it's painting, sketching, or sculpting, traditional art has been a fundamental means of self-expression throughout human history. From ancient cave paintings to modern masterpieces, art allows individuals to visually communicate their inner worlds.

- **Fashion**: The clothes we wear can serve as a canvas for self-expression and show off our personalities, interests, and beliefs. Fashion is not only a form of personal expression but can also be a statement of individuality and freedom.

- **Music**: Playing an instrument or even just singing can provide a powerful outlet for emotional expression. Songs convey personal experiences and beliefs through poetry and melody, which can allow the listeners to connect with the artist's self-expression.

- **Theater**: Acting enables individuals to step into the shoes of another person, while also using their own experiences to portray different, yet believable, characters. Whether on stage or in public speaking engagements, theatrical performances can offer a platform for self-expression and personal growth.

- **Writing**: Whether writing blog posts, novels, or even poetry, writing can allow individuals to articulate their thoughts, emotions, and experiences on paper.

Express Yourself at Open Forums/Town Meetings

Getting involved in your community is essential. This includes involving yourself in the politics and concerns of said community. While you're learning to express yourself and communicate effectively, consider engaging with others at open forums or town meetings.

Both online and offline engagement can bring incredible change and your voice matters. Even in the middle of our fast-paced digital world, town hall meetings can offer a great opportunity to participate in local government.

They also provide a platform to empower citizens in a way that allows them to connect with elected representatives, voice their concerns, and actively participate in shaping their communities.

These types of meetings have been a part of the United States since the seventeenth century, particularly in the New England region. They are seen as an example of a deliberative democracy by bringing together community members to discuss concerns with the decision-makers. The importance of townhall meetings include:

- **Inclusive and transparent decision-making:** Town hall meetings are open to the public, which allows citizens to observe the decision-making process first-hand. It also gives citizens the opportunity to hold elected representatives accountable for their actions. Individuals in a community are encouraged to speak up and participate.

- **Direct dialogue and feedback:** Since you are encouraged to participate, you will likely be talking directly to your elected officials and have the ability to express your concerns directly to them and receive direct responses. This sort of two-way interaction can lead to a political system that is fairer for everyone.

- **Education and awareness:** Town hall meetings are also great as they can educate the community about how local government operates, including their policy-making, budget allocations, and resource management. By attending this kind of meeting, you can gain awareness and equip yourself with the knowledge needed to make well-founded suggestions and advocate for realistic policies and changes.

Key Takeaways:

Effective communication strategies are one of the biggest parts of breathing positivity into the relationships you will have across all facets of your life. From open dialogue to active listening and respectfully expressing your needs, communication can truly enhance the understanding you have with others and strengthen the connection you have with them.

By clearly communicating personal needs and limits, you can nurture a mutual respect with others, minimize conflict, and create a supportive environment conducive to growth and happiness. Embracing and respecting differences in opinion and boundaries is essential for cultivating understanding and harmony within all relationships—including those with our neighbors and community as a whole. Diversity enriches interactions and allows for a culture of acceptance and empathy. Embrace your differences with one another but be consistent in upholding boundaries, as it reinforces personal values and shows self-respect because you're prioritizing self-care and ensuring your own well-being as well. In situations where boundaries are repeatedly violated, establishing consequences may be necessary. Know your limits and make sure others do as well.

Finally, don't be afraid to go beyond boundaries to really express yourself. Of course, the goal is to learn how to effectively listen to others, but it's also the goal to learn how to appropriately express yourself and all you have to offer. You can't build a stronger community if you don't know what you have to offer others in the way of relationships. Make sure that you show off your passions—you never know when others may share them. And don't be afraid to bare your soul—try expressing yourself through art, writing, music, and your clothing choices to truly show who you are and what you're all about. Be yourself, and others in the community will embrace you. After all, what's the point of belonging if it's not you who they're accepting?

Chapter 3

Give Back

In human existence, the threads of our lives are interwoven with those of our communities. Just as we rely on the support and contributions of others, so too do we have a responsibility to give back and enrich the lives of those around us. The concept of "giving back" transcends charity, however. Instead, it embodies the spirit of compassion, solidarity, and overall collective well-being of the community as a whole. This chapter explores the profound impact of giving back on both individuals and communities, emphasizing the transformative power of truly engaging with your community. From volunteering time and resources to advocating for social justice, each act of generosity serves to positively change the world around us. Join us as we delve into the importance of giving back and discover how acts of kindness can ignite a ripple effect of compassion, resilience, and hope within our communities.

Donate Blood

According to statistical research, every two seconds, someone in the United States requires a blood transfusion. In this, hospitals rely on the goodness of others to get the blood they need, when they need it.

Being a donator of blood is not only great because it helps others, but it can also be beneficial to you. Here are some of the things that you receive as a blood donor:

- **A free health screening:** By going to donate blood, you are basically getting a mini-physical. For free. Your vital signs will be checked, including blood pressure and heart rate. You will be screened for high blood pressure and issues such as heart arrhythmia like atrial fibrillation. Additionally, you will also be screened for diseases that you could be unaware of.

- **A healthier heart and vascular system:** Regular blood donation has been linked to lower blood pressure and a lower risk for heart attacks. There are a few connections to this. For example, if your hemoglobin is too high, blood donation helps to lower the viscosity—or thickness—of the blood. This type of issue has been linked to blood clots, heart attacks, and stroke. Frequent donations can minimize these concerns.

- **A happier, longer life:** According to research, just one blood donation can save up to three lives. People donate because it feels good to help others, and this sort of altruistic mentality and volunteering has been linked to positive health outcomes, which include a lower risk for depression.

- **A free (and calorie-free) snack:** After each blood donation, you get some juice and cookies! Want a bonus? Did you know that it takes an average person's body 500 or more calories to replace each blood donation? This means that whatever you eat after your next donation is going to be basically calorie-free (as far as effects go).

Contribute to a Food Bank

The truth is, in life, there are loads of things many of us think we can't go without. However, the truth of the matter is these are sometimes luxury items. In truth, there are very few things we cannot go without. The things we absolutely need are generally those we often take for granted. The biggest of those? Having a full meal every morning, afternoon, and evening.

The unfortunate truth is that people in many communities are going to bed hungry each and every night while food insecurity runs rampant in parts of the United States and worldwide. By donating to food banks, we can contribute to the overall well-being of our communities in more ways than we may realize.

Donating money to a food pantry is a way to make a huge impact by giving back to the community and supporting those in need. Food insecurity is a widespread issue worldwide, and it affects millions of individuals and families every day. By contributing to a food pantry, you directly address this pressing issue and provide essential sustenance to individuals who are facing hunger.

One of the most significant advantages of donating to a food pantry is its immediate impact. Some donations (at other charities) take time to see results, whereas food donation organizations give directly to families who need support, providing them with immediate relief. Food banks take up canned goods and non-perishables, which we will discuss later, but they also take up monetary donations, which is what we will discuss in this section.

It's a great thing to donate food directly, however monetary donations can go a lot further. In fact, each donated dollar can become several meals for someone in need. This is achievable because many food banks work with major manufacturers, retailers, and farmers directly, meaning they can get things for a cheaper price and truly stretch your dollars! In fact, although non-perishables such as canned foods and dry items like pasta and rice are great, and a vital part of nutrition, no one can sustain themselves on non-perishables alone. Providing communities with meals isn't just about providing food. It's about providing healthy food! In order to do this, balanced meals should be considered. This includes fresh fruit, vegetables, dairy, lean proteins, etc. These items can't be donated due to shelf-life. However, by working directly with farmers, food banks are able to ensure that these healthy fruits and vegetables can make it to the plates of families in need. Did you know that over one hundred billion pounds of food is wasted every year? When you donate your money to a food bank, you are also helping them work with organizations to minimize that waste and create a more sustainable world.

Collect Cans of Food or Non-Perishables

Although the last section may seem as though you shouldn't donate non-perishables and only donate your money—that isn't true! If you, your family, your friends, or anyone in your community has canned or dry foods that aren't being used—absolutely donate them! Donating wholesome food for human consumption diverts food waste from landfills and puts food on the table for families—specifically those in need. By donating your non-perishables you can:

- **Reduce environmental impact**: Donating food actually helps serve two purposes for bettering communities, though one is less obvious than the other, and that is reducing environmental impact. Aside from the immediate benefit to the members of your community, the planet can also benefit greatly as well. Think about it, the less unspoiled food that gets thrown away, the less unspoiled food that is sent to a landfill where it ultimately goes to waste.

- **Help community members thrive:** When people are able to eat, they become healthy enough to play their part as active and engaged members of their communities. We are only as strong as our weakest link, right? Ensuring everyone has enough food to eat not only supports local communities and economies, but society on a larger scale. Through food donations, communities can ensure that children and teenagers are healthy enough to attend school where they get an education and obtain social skills. They can also grow properly when not experiencing malnutrition. Food donations also ensure that adults have the health and energy needed to go to work and contribute to society as well as support their families, and that seniors get the nutrition they need to stay healthy as they get older and live longer.

Donating food isn't that difficult. There are many food banks and food pantries that will happily take your donations. Unfortunately, it isn't something people consider as often as they should. So, get involved, donate, and lead by example to get others involved!

Contribute to Your Community Library

There are a couple of ways you can contribute to your community library, both of which can aid your community. A library is merely a collection of information resources, in print or in other forms, that are made accessible for reading or study. Libraries can act as hubs for learning because they typically offer both past and present information.

Libraries have been around for a very long time, the first library was recorded in the seventh century BCE in Iraq. Before the advent of online search engines like Google, which is the most commonly used search engine, people with questions commonly turned to the most reliable source they knew—and that was their library, whether public, private, or in an academic setting. Libraries are important for several reasons, namely:

- **They provide public spaces to learn:** They are safe spaces where everyone is welcome and a place where everyone belongs (which is at the core of what human beings are designed to want—belonging). Modern libraries are seen as cultural and community hubs that draw groups eager to learn in one space. Access to these types of spaces is so important, and the fact that most are free is equally important as they provide communities with much-needed resources.

- **They ensure that informational material is readily**

available—for free: Public libraries play an important role in providing safe, accessible, and free information to communities. At a public library, money is no factor because every resource is free of charge. Public libraries provide resources such as books, internet access, and educational and professional training materials. Individuals can truly count on their libraries to provide them with information on questions they might not have been able to find otherwise. Because libraries offer various kinds of books, they can be hubs for not only information but entertainment as well.

- **They provide free internet connectivity:** Our lives are all so digital these days. Because of this, the fact that visitors have the ability to enjoy free Wi-Fi is a huge benefit. In fact, this could mean the difference between someone being able to work or not. For example, someone who cannot afford Internet can quickly go to a library and apply for a job. There are also opportunities for people to work remotely in libraries by utilizing their free Wi-Fi.

- **They typically have well-trained human resources:** Libraries in the United States are run on the shoulders of librarians. They are more than just a warm body to watch over all the books. In fact, they can truly add to the overall experience at a library. They typically are well-versed with a ton of knowledge and experience. If you're researching a topic, they can generally point you in the right direction of information. If you're looking for a book recommendation, they can oftentimes refer you to something you will really enjoy by just asking a few questions about your likes. They are the ones that catalog books and put them back on the shelves, sure—but that isn't the reason they're so smart! Most librarians attend college. In fact, many libraries require their librarians to have a degree.

- **They are a great place to socialize and network:** This guide is all about socializing and networking! Being part of a community! In today's world, networking is one thing that enables a community to grow, both socially and economically. Although you shouldn't strike up a conversation just anywhere in a library (people are trying to work and study, after all! Shh!), you can still get to know people who have the same interests you do by going to the library to find them. This is usually done quietly as you see someone reading a favorite book (or asking for a recommendation), or at one of the various events libraries put on for the community!

All in all, it's pretty evident that libraries are important. But where do they get their funds? What about their resources? The answer lies in grants, donations, and governmental budgets. This is where you can help! There are several ways you can help your community library, such as:

- **Offering money:** Libraries always need money; for books, for new resources, to keep the lights on, and to do fun and engaging events! Offer up a monetary donation if you feel moved to help out! They will put it to good use!

- **Sponsoring a read-a-thon or event:** A lot of businesses can take advantage of events at libraries in exchange for advertisement opportunities! Many libraries offer sponsorship spots for read-a-thons or other events (or displays inside the library) so that they can raise enough money. In exchange, they offer to display businesses' names and logos. Consider this if you're a business owner wanting some community outreach!

- **Donating your books:** While it is super easy to just donate your old books online—shipping the books off for free and being done—think about donating them locally. Even if your books aren't needed (due to age, condition, or enough copies already being at the library), consider Little Free Library instead of shipping off your books to a big box location for profit. Little Free Library is an organization that allows you to donate used books for others to read. These libraries are generally placed inside little "book houses" outside of libraries, schools, churches, etc. so that people can access literature for free.

- **Donating your time:** Libraries are always looking for volunteers. Ask for opportunities to help out (on your schedule) and they will be sure to have something for you!

Offer to Read to the Elderly

Going beyond libraries, it's important to note that there remains an importance of general reading—and that is first introduced to us as a whole when we're children. While the importance of promoting reading among children does get the majority of attention, there are plenty of benefits for adults, especially seniors.

In fact, reading is linked with a number of positive outcomes for older adults, including enhanced memory retention, better decision-making skills, a reduction in stress, better sleep patterns, and delayed onset of Alzheimer's and dementia. Not to mention the fact that can be quite enjoyable as well.

However, the unfortunate truth is that reading can get harder as we age. In fact, one study shows that at least 25 percent of seniors hit a roadblock when it comes to reading for themselves. Luckily there are some simple ways to overcome these obstacles. E-reading devices (such as Kindles) with backlit screens and adjustable font sizes are particularly useful for seniors with vision problems, as well as for those suffering from arthritis and other challenges to dexterity. Older adults who may not be as comfortable with technology have adaptive methods that they can try, such as large print books, reading lights, magnifiers, book holders, and audiobooks. All of these can aid in overcoming those obstacles.

Another way that seniors can overcome these obstacles is to have someone read to them. If you know a senior who suffers from a cognitive impairment that impedes their ability to read, consider reading to them. Also, consider going to a facility where seniors reside and offer your assistance. This can be a great way to form a connection, make you feel better for helping someone in need, and can bring a lot of enjoyment to the senior. Think about it, not only are they becoming engrossed in a wonderful story, but they also have company. This can affect them two-fold.

Volunteer at an Animal Shelter

Volunteering with animals in general can be an incredibly rewarding experience. Not only do you get to help care for and protect some of the most vulnerable creatures in the world, but you also get to form close bonds while you're helping them.

Volunteering to help animals can take many different forms, from working at a local shelter to providing foster care for homeless pets. No matter what type of volunteering you choose to do with the shelter, there are many benefits to be had.

Make a Difference

The most obvious reason to volunteer to work with animals is to make a difference in their lives. Pets in shelters and rescues often come from difficult backgrounds. Some have been through a lot in just a short amount of time. By volunteering your time and energy to help care for them, you can make a real difference to their health and their future well-being.

Animals in shelters and rescues rely on volunteers for everything. This includes walking, getting exercise, socializing, and even grooming. Without volunteers, nearly all of the pets at shelters would go without even the most basic of care.

Great Way to Exercise

There are a ton of great benefits to volunteering at an animal shelter, and getting out and getting good exercise is a wonderful one for your overall health. If you're looking for a way to get out of the house and get some fresh air, volunteering at a shelter really is a great option. By walking dogs and exercising them, you can get your cardio in.

Meet New People and Make New Friends

While you're out walking with the pets at the shelter, you not only get great exercise but also have a great bonding opportunity, which the animals at the shelter likely need very much. Beyond just bonding with the pets, though, volunteering is also a great way to meet new people and make new friends. When you volunteer at a shelter or rescue center, you can meet other people who share your love and passion for animals. This can lead to developing great friendships in your community while doing something good for your community and making a difference within it.

Learn New Skills

If you volunteer with animals, you have a great opportunity to potentially learn new skills as well. Many shelters and rescues offer training programs for those who volunteer. You can learn about animal care, handling, first aid, and more. It is also a great way to learn about the inner workings of the shelter and how they allocate their resources.

Ultimately, there are abundant benefits to volunteering at a local shelter. Overall, just knowing that you're making a difference in your community and helping animals that need it is the greatest benefit of all.

Give Your Time to the Soup Kitchen

In many communities, soup kitchens are some of the few places where the homeless can get a free hot meal and a sack lunch without judgment or discrimination. If your community doesn't have one, contemplate starting one—or finding out if your community offers "warming" centers. Although "warming centers" don't operate all the time, they can be quite beneficial when they do, since they generally operate when it's cold or the weather is harsh.

Regardless of whether you volunteer at a soup kitchen, a warming center, or something else that helps the homeless, know that the kitchen or supplies generally rely solely on the generosity of the people in the community. They run almost entirely on donations and volunteers.

There are many reasons to volunteer at an establishment that aids the homeless. These reasons are:

- **It's gratifying:** Volunteering may not make you rich monetarily since you do it without pay, but it gives you something more valuable than money can ever bring you. There is an incredible amount of satisfaction and happiness that can come from helping others.

- **You make a difference:** Food is a basic need no matter how you spin it and knowing that you're helping people with that basic need is critical. Also, knowing that you have helped someone not go hungry is a good feeling—and it really does help.

- **You can meet like-minded people:** It is important to

get to know people with similar passions. Surrounding yourself with like-minded and kind people is essential in loving your community, and this is a great benefit of meeting people through homeless shelter volunteering!

- **It's more than giving back:** As humans, it is our responsibility to help the more vulnerable people in our communities. We are only as strong as our weak and hungry. By helping out, you're helping lift people up in many more ways than just feeding them.

- **You can learn more about life and make relationships:** Part of meeting other people is learning about their lives and the stories they have been a part of—this can be the people you're serving or the people you're serving with. The experiences of every person you meet can teach you valuable lessons that you won't learn in books or movies. You can learn to drop your prejudices and stereotypes by volunteering, as well. You can learn to embrace people as they are as well as understand where they are coming from. It is a great opportunity to sympathize with sorrows and celebrate victories with people you've newly met and grow potentially long-term relationships.

- **You can learn more skills:** There are lots of things you can learn as a volunteer. If cooking is not your thing, you can learn it. If you don't want to learn, that's fine, too! There are many areas where the expertise you do have is needed. You can wash dishes, serve the food, stock shelves, or even pick up food donations from homes, churches, etc. in the area.

- **You're setting a good example:** If you have kids or even siblings, chances are they look up to you as a role model. Role models are needed in life—not just by children. Helping those in need allows you to set a good example for the people who look up to you. It's a great opportunity to show others empathy and compassion.

- **It can be an opportunity for bonding:** Take your friends, your family, and even your young children. Volunteering can be a great opportunity to do something with the people you love while making a difference and teaching others how to become responsible citizens and human beings.

- **You can learn humility and appreciation:** Helping those in need helps put things into perspective for you. When you see people who are happy despite their negative situations, you can quickly realize that your problems are potentially not quite as bad as you thought. You can start to truly appreciate the things you do have: your home, your job, your family, and the fact that you can eat, wherever you want to, whenever you want to.

Coach or Tutor

Coaching can be a powerful tool. Leaders and role models are critical in the learning and development of people in communities, especially for children. Volunteering as a coach or a tutor is a great way to level up the community (as well as your involvement in it).

Young learners look up to a variety of role models and adults throughout their formative years. Role models end up shaping how they behave, the relationships they have, and the decisions they make. For many children, the most important role models are their parents, teachers (including tutors), and coaches. Having a good role model is extremely important for children and their development. Being a coach or a tutor can truly inspire children to stay motivated, display good behavior, make better life choices, and achieve higher goals. By being a coach or a tutor, you can help the community by helping the youth within it. This will allow you to love your community even more.

Donate What You No Longer Need

Everyone has had that moment when they can't quite close that overstuffed drawer or squeeze that last shirt into their closet. When these things start happening, it's time to downsize. As we discussed earlier in this guide, a lot of organizations rely heavily on donations. This can go beyond that of food and clothing and come in the form of many other things. Of course, the thought of parting ways with old possessions may seem a little overwhelming but understand that there may also be a sense of relief and satisfaction once it is actually complete. Some benefits of donating what you no longer need include:

- **Decluttering your home**: When you start to have difficulty getting through your house or finding things because of all the clutter, definitely consider decluttering your home. This is a wonderful benefit of donating things you no longer need. Because once you have fewer things, you have much fewer items to get in the way to navigate through.

- **Eliminating storage costs:** Renting storage spaces to free up room in your home can become quite a costly endeavor. Monthly fees can quickly accumulate. Redirecting this money toward more meaningful purposes is a wise choice considering you can just as easily donate your extra items!

- **Boost selling potential:** Another benefit is the selling potential of your home. If you ever decide to list your property, showcasing your home in a clutter-free environment is essential. A tidy, spacious home can truly expedite the selling process and potentially increase your property's value.

- **Promoting environmental responsibility:** Donating unwanted furniture instead of discarding it helps reduce waste and supports reuse. By giving items a second life in another household or repurposing them creatively, you can contribute to sustainability efforts. Just because you're finished with it, doesn't mean it's finished serving a purpose. You might be surprised how much life can be breathed into items you may think are too worn out for anyone else. Don't forget that even if the full item cannot be used, it could be repurposed or even salvaged for parts.

- **Creating teachable moments:** Involving children or other loved ones in the donation process can help foster empathy and compassion. Allowing children to select items for donation and participate in delivering them can truly reinforce the importance of giving back to the community and to those who may need the items more.

- **Maximizing tax benefits:** Another excellent benefit of donating items is that doing so can really give you a significant tax deduction. By keeping track of donation receipts you can itemize deductions in order to capitalize on potential savings during tax season.

- **Supporting those in need:** There is one particularly significant benefit to donating and that's supporting others in the community. Donating items such as books, clothing, toys, and appliances not only prevents them from going to waste but also benefits people in your neighborhood. Depending on the item and who you donate to, you could potentially really give something to someone who truly needs it. Your contributions can make a meaningful difference in someone else's life.

Pick Up Trash and Promote Recycling

Arm yourself with bags, gloves, litter pickers, and a sense of purpose to get to work and clean up your community! Cleanups are good for raising awareness. However, there have been critics who suggest that they do little to address the problem. This is because they do not address the root causes of pollution. For example, cleaning a beach is not exactly turning the tide. The tide will just come in again, and more plastic cups/bottles, straws, grocery bags, and discarded items will be brought along with it. The ideal situation would be that we could reduce unnecessary plastics at the source and even take it a step further by designing less harmful products and developing more recycling processes. But the truth of the matter is that picking up trash is still effective. It not only raises awareness, as stated before, but it also means that every piece of trash you pick up and recycle is one extra item not deposited in a landfill. It's also removing one item that could be potentially hazardous for wildlife. Cleaning up restores habitats.

So, even if there is merit to the argument that the source of the problem needs to be tackled, there is no denying that volunteer cleanup projects protect wildlife. They can also create a bit of momentum, raise awareness, and save habitats that may be threatened. In fact, it could be concluded that picking up trash is critical to make sure the community maintains awareness while working together to seek a long-term solution.

Plastic pollution of our rivers and seas is a monumental disaster. It has global consequences and is composed of multiple sources; so, coming up with a long-term solution may be a little difficult. However, public engagement from the community is critical to encourage behavior change. This can aid in some of the source issues but also allow for momentum to put pressure on government entities and businesses to take more action. The truth is, everyone can play a role in creating a solution and it will take everyone to make a significant impact—starting with you. So, get out there, pick up some garbage, and spread the word!

Key Takeaways:

In this chapter, we have learned that giving back to our community is not only one of the best ways to love our community more but to also show that love in a way that causes it to flourish for the better.

First off, we discussed how community engagement is vital to giving back. Giving back to your community isn't just about charity; it's about rebranding the word to truly mean solidarity and collective well-being. If one community member is struggling, we all do. We should pull each other from the trenches and act in generosity, no matter how big or small the action. Each act can contribute to positive change and strengthen your community.

Efforts such as volunteering offer numerous benefits, including personal fulfillment, skill development, and social connections. Whether you're coaching, tutoring, or assisting at a soup kitchen/homeless shelter, your time and effort can make a huge difference in the lives of others. You are supporting people's basic needs. For example, donating items such as food, clothing, and household goods can truly aid in maintaining dignity, happiness, and health in your community. You will be supporting in particular those who are struggling and rely on the aid of community organizations. When it comes to donating, remember, even if it's things you have lying around that you just want to dispose of because they're taking up too much room, they can be something of a treasured need to someone else. By donating, you are reducing waste and promoting the reuse of those items that may otherwise just end up in a landfill. So not only is donating contributing to someone in need, but it's also environmentally responsible, which is also a huge part of giving back. By recycling and participating in clean-up initiatives you help protect wildlife, preserve habitats, and raise awareness of pollution and landfills filling up too much of our precious land. Every effort counts toward creating a cleaner, healthier planet for future generations.

It's also up to you to set a precedent for giving back if you wish to change your community. The idea is that giving back inspires others to do the same. Whether it's donating goods, volunteering, or participating in community clean-up efforts, your actions can inspire positive change and encourage others to join in.

Chapter 4

Keep Yourself and Others Healthy

This chapter is all about keeping yourself—and others—healthy. In this chapter, we explore ways to keep ourselves and our communities healthy through engaging activities and innovative projects. We also delve into various activities that not only promote individual well-being but also foster stronger bonds within our communities themselves. From discovering new hobbies to participating in community gardening projects, there are countless opportunities to make a positive impact on the collective health of our communities, as well as our personal well-being.

Throughout this chapter, we'll highlight the importance of staying active, connecting with nature, supporting local initiatives, and building stronger community networks. Whether you're embarking on a new adventure with friends or volunteering to enhance the well-being of your neighborhood, there's something for everyone in the quest for a healthier lifestyle.

Start a Community Group

Ready to take your shared interests to the next level? By starting a community group centered around activities that you enjoy you can deepen your connections with others while also making a positive impact in your neighborhood and feeding the health of your psyche as well as that of others around you. And depending on what kind of community group you start, you can potentially even benefit your physical health, too. Whether you're passionate about cooking, hiking, photography, or any other hobby, forming a community group encircling your passions allows you to share your enthusiasm for those hobbies with like-minded individuals and create a supportive network of folks in your own backyard.

Do Activities You Enjoy

As adults, we all have hobbies. There may be some that you already enjoy participating in whether it be by yourself or with loved ones. However, exploring brand new activities or hobbies can be an exciting way to enjoy life and socialize and grow bonds with our loved ones. It creates memories and you begin to associate these fun and new experiences with your loved ones which can truly strengthen your relationships.

Whether it's learning a new skill, embarking on a creative project together, or engaging in a shared interest that neither of you has tried before, trying a new hobby can really improve your connection with a loved one, especially if you decide to create a community group based around your passion! So, find out what activities you enjoy that you might want to share with others! It really could help improve your mental and physical health, no matter what you choose! Some hobbies you might consider making a community group out of are:

- **Cooking or baking:** Experimenting with new recipes or baking homemade treats that you saw online or on TV can be fun and delicious.

- **Gardening:** Gardening is not only a relaxing hobby but can also lead to beautiful results. Hint, you can even turn a community garden into a community group! Or get involved with a local group at church to really make it happen!

- **Painting or drawing:** Explore your artistic side by taking up painting, drawing, or other forms of visual art. You can create your own art or attend art classes. Now there are even "painting with a twist" classes that involve wine and other fun elements.

- **Hiking or nature walks:** Enjoy the great outdoors by going on hikes or nature walks in local parks or nature reserves. It's an excellent way to stay active and appreciate nature.

- **Photography:** Capture moments and memories by taking up photography. You can explore your surroundings and document your adventures together.

- **Playing musical instruments:** Learning an instrument can be difficult, but also incredibly rewarding! Studies have shown music to be incredibly beneficial for people. Even if you don't know how to play an instrument, you can potentially start a group for all skill levels and learn together!

- **Birdwatching:** Birdwatching can be a relaxing and educational hobby. Get a pair of binoculars and observe the various bird species in your area. You can also put up a few feeders nearby and enjoy them up close, as well.

- **Knitting:** Learning how to make your own garments or blankets can be fun and can give you and your group a chance to catch up and talk while you make them!

- **Wine or beer tasting:** If you're of legal drinking age and appreciate beer or wine, you can explore different wineries or breweries with your loved ones—or maybe even start crafting your own as part of your group!

- **Puzzle-solving:** Work on jigsaw puzzles, crosswords, or brain-teasers in a group. Puzzle-solving can be a mentally stimulating and enjoyable pastime. There are subscription boxes you can sign up for, too, so make it a monthly ritual to solve a new one together with your group!

- **Dancing:** Learn different dance styles like ballroom, salsa, or swing dancing. You can take classes or learn from YouTube—or if you're already a pro, you can teach the group!

- **Book club:** Start a book club and read and discuss books together. It's an excellent way to share your thoughts and insights on various literature—and this can even open up the door to more in-depth and meaningful discussions.

- **Yoga or meditation:** Self-care is important, and combining yoga and meditation is a great two-for-one. By combining these, you can practice self-care and participate in great quality time with your group. Use it as a way to stay healthy and reduce stress, and if you want to make it extra fun, bring a loved one along to a class (or, again, if you're already a pro—teach it!)

- **Volunteer work:** Find a cause or organization you are passionate about and sign up to volunteer. It's a meaningful way to give back to the community together.

- **Stargazing:** Bring the chairs and the snacks and spend evenings stargazing and identifying constellations. Consider investing in a telescope for a more in-depth celestial exploration and keep track of events happening in your area.

- **Model car building:** Pick up an old craft like building model cars! It's possible this can hold some nostalgia behind it, but sharing your passion with fellow car enthusiasts is definitely a fun, engaging, and satisfying option.

- **Home improvement:** Collaborate on home improvement projects or DIY renovations. This can be a productive and satisfying way to upgrade your living space. Branch out, too, and potentially earn extra cash in the meantime.

- **Travel:** Plan and take trips together with a group. Make sure you're exploring new places, cultures, and cuisines since this is all about trying new things together and truly experiencing things with one another. Traveling can create unforgettable shared experiences.

Remember that the key to a successful shared hobby (or in this case, a community group hobby) is to choose activities that all parties can enjoy and that align with your interests and abilities. Really make sure that whatever you choose, you're able to experience it with multiple people and that you are able to stay consistent and keep at it!

Consider Spiritual Community Groups

A Bible (or spiritual) community group can also be a great thing to start if you're the spiritual type. These types of groups can have immense significance in the lives of believers, offering a supportive environment for spiritual growth, fellowship, and accountability. These groups, often formed within churches or religious organizations, provide a space where everyone can come together to study scriptures, pray, and share their journey with one another. It truly can be an incredible community-building exercise.

One of the primary benefits of participating in a community group of this type is the opportunity to deepen one's understanding of scripture, while also sharing your spiritual journey (and listening to others share theirs). Through group discussions, members can gain insights into the meaning of scripture, explore different interpretations, and apply religious teachings to their daily lives. This collaborative approach to studying the Bible (or other scripture) not only enriches individual understanding but also fosters a sense of unity and shared purpose among group members.

In addition to growing intellectually and starting to understand scripture, these community groups can offer a sense of belonging and fellowship that is essential for spiritual nourishment and growth. As members build relationships with one another, they find encouragement, support, and companionship, and begin a bit of a spiritual journey together. These kinds of community groups are great because they exemplify what everyone wants in a community in general. During times of joy and celebration, someone is there to celebrate with you! During moments of struggle and hardship—someone is there to be a source of strength and comfort! Truly, once you develop a relationship with these people you learn to bear one another's burdens. And this really can be therapeutic and fulfilling to those on a spiritual journey.

Moreover, these kinds of community groups serve as places of accountability where group members can challenge and encourage one another to live out their faith authentically. Through open and honest dialogue, individuals are held accountable to biblical principles and are challenged to grow in their relationship with God and others. You are generally assigned passages and just like a book club are expected to participate in discussing what you learned and how it can be applied to your everyday life. This mutual accountability can really encourage spiritual maturity and help individuals stay grounded in their faith amidst life's challenges and temptations.

Finally, religious community groups play a vital role in outreach, providing a platform for members to share the love of their spiritual relationship with others. As the group grows in faith and unity, its impact extends beyond its own members to the wider community, as members are inspired and equipped to share religious teachings with those around them. By embodying the love and teachings scripture offers, community groups become beacons of hope and transformation in a world that is sometimes—and sometimes too often—plagued by division and despair.

Plow and Seed a Community Garden

Ever tried getting involved in a community garden? Ever heard of one? If not, it's time to jump in or even kick-start one yourself!

Why? Because community gardening can have many benefits for people, neighborhoods, and the environment in general. Just having one community garden can strengthen community ties and maybe even help curb crime rates. Community gardens can also help people in need.

Plus, these gardens make neighborhoods look nicer and offer chances for folks to pick up some new skills. So, what is a community garden?

It's like a green oasis where neighbors join forces to plant flowers, fruits, vegetables, and herbs. They're quite popular in some cities, but there is still plenty of space for them to become more prominent. Community gardens may be established by organizations such as churches, non-profits, clubs, and municipalities. Even private landowners can participate if they choose to donate a portion of their property to community garden efforts! But regardless of who establishes it, it is a great way to get involved in your community and learn to love it a little more. It truly has benefits for people and the community at large, some of which include:

- **Beautifying the landscape:** In many urban neighborhoods, there are vacant lots that have fallen into disuse. They could be filled with garbage, which can be a huge eyesore and a danger. If these are used for gardens, you are left with a green living space where birds and insects can thrive. This sort of community outreach can do away with vacant lots, and their presence may even cause property values to increase due to all the benefits they can offer.

- **Making fresh produce more accessible:** In many urban neighborhoods, obtaining regular, fresh produce without having to drive further out can be costly. This means that fresh produce is not as accessible to middle- and low-income households, making a nutritiously round diet not as accessible. Community gardens are an effective way of alleviating this issue.

- **Promoting healthier lifestyles:** When people have more access to fresh fruits and vegetables, they have a greater opportunity to be healthier. Community gardening leads to healthier lifestyles because it improves diets and encourages regular exercise—gardening itself can offer quite the workout. Having the opportunity to work outside is a wonderful way to help avoid being sedentary, which is a major contributor to obesity.

- **Cleaning up the environment:** Plants add oxygen to the air, and that oxygen is then breathed in by people. Those same plants also filter out air pollution and further absorb rainwater, which means that there is less runoff in the streets. This leads to fewer pollutants being washed into rivers and streams. Also, bonus points for community gardeners who practice composting, as this is an effective way of reducing waste. Tree trimmings, leaves, etc., can all be used as fertilizer.

- **Building stronger communities:** This entire guide is

about loving your community more. That means the people in it. By being involved in a community garden you gain the opportunity to connect with others on a one-on-one basis. Think about it, with a community garden, the people who reach out to you and volunteer their time could be people who might otherwise have been cooped up at home. In fact, you may even be that person. The truth of the matter is that social endeavors are everything, as stated earlier in this guide. Leading a solitary life is no way to live and if a community garden can bring people out to interact with one another, it can become a truly wonderful experience. Additionally, stronger and tighter-knit communities have lower crime rates, which is another extraordinary benefit of merely just getting to know one another through an outreach such as this.

- **Opportunities for learning:** Educational opportunities are huge in community gardens. They can really be wonderful places for people to interact with others who may have different cultural, social, and religious backgrounds. There is also the potential, by working together in the garden, that you can learn new techniques and more about plants in general. Children can even benefit from learning about food growth and nutrition in a hands-on learning experience.

- **Relieving stress:** Let's face it, life is stressful. Most people go from one activity to the next with a never-ending to-do list. Gardening is a great way to slow down, connect with nature and others, and create a whole new approach to life.

Put Up Animal Feeders

Animal feeders give you the opportunity to observe the wonders of nature and take a little break from the hustle and bustle of daily life. Access to feeders can teach a plethora of new and engaging information by giving you the ability to identify species and learn the importance of caring for nature. With a steady supply of food in your feeders, you can have animals in your backyard year-round.

There are loads of benefits to feeding animals in your own backyard that go beyond your joy in looking at them. There are many benefits for birds in particular. When we think of wild birds, we generally think about them only benefiting from backyard feeders during certain times of the year. However, the truth of the matter is that they need year-round food sources. And when the population goes up in the summer, there's a greater demand for limited food sources. The more you are able to feed birds during nesting season, the less time the mother bird will need to stay away from the nest foraging for food. This can truly help younger bird species survive by having their mother there more often to protect them.

Studies also show that birds in areas with feeders are in overall better health than birds in places without feeders. This means that just feeding birds makes a difference for the future of wild birds. Studies also show that there is a likely impact of bird feeders on the stress levels of birds. This research shows that the stress levels wild birds might experience decrease by just having that food security.

And just as you can decrease the stress levels of birds—they can also reduce yours. One of the most relaxing sounds you can ever experience is the chirping of birds as they perch near your home.

People enjoy bird feeding as a soothing source of natural beauty and entertainment just outside their windows.

Host Exercise Sessions

Developing a gym community offers many benefits. A community can benefit from physical fitness by turning simple workouts into enjoyable, sociable experiences. Build a strong community in physical fitness by:

- **Connecting with others online:** Keep others informed and invite them to be involved in exercise sessions. This can be a workout at a home gym, a walk-a-thon in the neighborhood, or a session at a gym you frequent. Make it fun and get people involved. Whether you create a user-friendly website or active social media accounts, you can reach your community folk wherever they are! Maintaining your connection with others and engaging with them in a way that encourages them to get fit with you not only allows you to get to know others but also gets people excited to work out and grow a healthier community in general.

- **Host community events:** A community bonds over commonalities, like similar interests or even just mutual goals. Hosting an event for exercise can connect people for a shared experience. Maybe your goal is to lose weight—or maybe it's just to tone up. Invite others who have the same goal to do an event with you! The more group events you host, the more memories, goals, and interests you create for your community members.

- **Encourage feedback:** Involvement, engagement, and collaboration are key community components, as they connect everyone. Encouraging your neighbors to give feedback or make requests allows for collaborative communication and builds a sense of togetherness. The more people are engaging with your efforts to host exercise sessions, the stronger their bond with the event/group/session. You can receive feedback by establishing regular times to provide suggestions or by giving everyone an anonymous survey. Collaborate and enjoy the camaraderie!

- **Foster a welcoming environment:** Most importantly, if you want to host an exercise session, make sure that you're welcoming—especially if you want others to continue to show. Keeping people engaged in a fitness journey can be difficult, and the more comfortable and confident everyone is, the better results you will have!

Support Local Farmers' Markets

No matter if you're looking for a small change in scenery during your weekly shopping trips, if you want to support small businesses, or if you're just trying to find better food to stay healthy—local farmers' markets have you covered. Shopping at your local farmers' market comes with some pretty great benefits, which include:

- **Strengthening your community and local economy:**

Studies show that on average, only ten cents of each dollar for food goes back to the farmer who first harvested it. The other ninety cents go to corporations for packaging, marketing, and transportation. However, farmers who sell directly to consumers receive eighty cents of each food dollar. That money is then put back into the local community, boosting the local economy.

- **The produce is at peak flavor and nutrition:** Not only is buying locally an economic benefit for your community, but you also benefit twofold: getting to know who is growing your food, and eating fresher, healthier food. This is considered a win-win!

- **Trying something new:** Sometimes you want to try something new that is different from your predictable, boring grocery store. Going to a farmers' market allows you to do just that. Additionally, farmers' markets tend to have more of the novel products that you might not expect at a typical grocery store. Perhaps it's a food you've never heard of—or maybe just something you haven't tried yet. When you do find something novel or unique at a local market, the experience can be a bit of an adventure. So, get out there and try something new!

Join Parks and Recreation Committees

All work and no play makes everyone really dull! That's why joining parks and recreation committees and volunteering are excellent experiences! Joining up with your local chapter is a great way to share your time, talents, and enthusiasm with your community—and committee members generally get to engage with community members in exercise activities, meaning better health and exercise are coming your way, too! Please note that these are generally working committees. Applicants should be willing to give time to monthly meetings and committee projects or events if they intend to join. If you aren't looking for quite the commitment, consider volunteering for projects instead—or even events that your local chapter holds (or suggest some to your local parks and recreation department). This can be something like easter egg hunts, family picnic days, father/daughter dances, mother/son dances, or community play days.

Getting involved in parks and recreation is a fun endeavor. It can be really rewarding because you're not only giving to your community, but you're also staying active! And the good news? It doesn't matter what kind of project you get involved in, they're all sure to contribute to making you and your community healthier! The truth is, there are a lot of programs within parks and recreation that could use all the help they can get! These ventures include "Adopt-A" programs such as:

- **Adopt-A-Mile:** This is a great opportunity where you simply get involved in such a way that you "adopt a mile". So, you—or your group—will be assigned a mile stretch to clean every so often (generally once every three months or so). This is also a great opportunity for businesses because oftentimes the city will advertise who has adopted the mile, providing great exposure.

- **Adopt-A-Greenway:** This is very similar to the "Adopt-A-Mile" program, but instead, you can adopt a "greenway", such as a stretch of park or sidewalk area. Generally, the city provides necessary supplies in exchange for your work. They also tend to advertize for whomever "adopts" this section of the city!

- **Adopt-A-Stream:** Do you like wading through water? This is a great one, especially for the warmer months! Adopting a stream allows volunteers to learn how to properly take care of a stream. Since this involves water and can be more dangerous, some training is usually required. However, it's a great opportunity to explore nature and help out your parks and recreation department!

Other parks and recreation activities you can get yourself involved in include trail maintenance at some of your community parks, or trailheads), leading educational programs (especially if you have a skill you would like to donate such as wildlife management, or botany!), gardening, and coaching a sports league. The opportunities really are endless when it comes to a multi-faceted entity such as the Parks and Recreation Department. You can choose to volunteer your time and expertise on a regular basis or sporadically. No matter what you choose, they could definitely use you! And by doing so you're keeping yourself—and others—happy and healthy and truly working to make your community a better place.

Plant Trees

Planting trees can go a long way in our communities. Most often we plant trees to provide shade and make our landscapes even more beautiful. While these are great benefits, trees also provide other, less obvious benefits.

Trees in general just make life a whole lot better. It has been shown that spending time around trees and green spaces reduces the amount of stress that we carry around with us in our daily lives. Patients in various hospitals have been shown to recover from surgery more quickly when their hospital room is near a pleasant view of trees, too. And in a similar facet, children have been shown to retain more information if their classrooms are located near greenery/trees; and there are even more benefits if they get to spend some time outdoors in those spaces.

Trees have been a benchmark to our lives for generations and are often taken for granted, even though they do so much for us and symbolize many significant events in our lives. In fact, trees are often planted as living memorials or reminders of loved ones or to commemorate significant events in our lives.

You may like to look at your trees or enjoy the shade they provide, but hopefully after reading this section of *How to Love Your Community*, you can appreciate them just a little more as well as understand that they're incredibly beneficial to your community.

Through careful planning, trees can be an asset to your entire community. We all know that tree-lined streets look better. Trees can even be placed in such a way as to screen unwanted views or noise from busy highways. They can do all this while also complementing the architecture or design of buildings of the entire neighborhood.

The benefits to our environment and our communities may be obvious to many, but when we think of trees in our own yards, the benefits may not be so clear. We may think that they don't benefit anyone but ourselves. We often think that we need to travel to a plot of land somewhere a little more central or shared to plant a tree (a courthouse, a park, or a greenway). But know that although you may own the trees on your property, your neighbors will still benefit from them.

Environmental

Trees bring forth a plethora of environmental benefits. Through evaporative cooling and reducing the amount of sunlight (because trees provide shade) that can reach parking lots and buildings, more trees can reduce the urban heat island effect. They also improve our air quality by producing more oxygen and filtering harmful dust and pollutants from the air we breathe. They also reduce the amount of stormwater runoff, which then reduces pollution in our waterways. Trees are an incredible resource and they benefit us as well as various species of wildlife that depend on them for their habitats (for food, protection, and even homes).

Economical

By being strategic with tree placement, you can reduce your cooling costs in the summer due to the shade that they can provide. Planting evergreen trees and shrubs around the foundation of your home can act as a windbreak to reduce the cooling effects of wintertime winds, as well. So, truly, there is value in a well-landscaped home. Professionals can help determine how best to landscape your home using trees. Hiring professional help can be costly, but the economic benefits of planting trees make them an investment!

Participate in Community Watch Programs

Surveys show that communities with community/neighborhood watch programs have less fear and anxiety about their homes being broken into or their children being kidnapped. Studies also show that there is a direct correlation between feeling safe and having some sort of watch program in place.

If your community/neighborhood hasn't implemented something like this, consider getting one started! Many adults are ready and willing to become active in their neighborhood if they're asked to. Many people are simply unaware of such programs or are daunted by the commitment.

Volunteer and Support Anti-Drug Coalitions

Throughout the country, there are many organizations that cater to the anti-drug movement. However, if your community has an anti-drug coalition, they take this even further. They work to reduce dependence on harmful and potentially lethal substances such as prescription drugs, alcohol, and tobacco. These local efforts, generally funded by your state governments, help get the word out about the dangers and consequences of substance abuse. They also provide the community with much-needed tools and resources to strengthen this cause. Some of their efforts include:

- **Providing take-back boxes for prescription drugs and conduct events:** They provide safe disposal and recycling of prescription drugs to ensure they don't fall into the wrong hands.

- **Providing lockboxes to community members for their prescription drugs:** The anti-drug coalition also provides free-of-charge lockboxes for prescription drugs so that you can lock up your medicine without worrying about others accessing it. This is especially needed in a household with teenagers or impressionable youth.

- **Educating individuals handling alcoholic beverage transactions:** They designate employees or volunteers to train alcohol vendors in proper safety in handling and distributing alcohol.

- **Monitoring current smoke-free ordinances to encourage enforcement:** They act as an enforcer to ensure that smoke-free campuses remain such with the help of the community as a whole.

- **Posting anti-drug, anti-alcohol, and anti-smoking billboards in the community:** A little advertising never hurt anyone. The anti-drug coalitions typically post advertisements to deter youth from engaging in harmful activities.

- **Offering a reward for information on illegal drug manufacturing:** This is a great incentive for people to "watch" what is happening in their community and provide information if they suspect illegal drug manufacturing in the area. Drugs destroy communities and it is important to keep them at bay before they become a widespread problem. With this incentive, they hope to do this in many states, especially in those communities with more risk.

- **Engaging youth to participate in drug, alcohol, and tobacco-free efforts:** The anti-drug coalition is involved in school events and even creates its own events for school-aged children and teenagers. They go beyond just speaking to children, though. While they commonly make speeches in schools around the United States, anti-drug coalition employees and volunteers also provide a fun and engaging environment for youth to learn and bond through various events, clubs, and outings.

Participate in Candy-Striping or Volunteer at a Nursing Home

Candy stripers are volunteer workers in the healthcare setting, and they play an essential role in providing care and support to patients in various medical settings. Candy stripers originated in the 1940s when a group of high school students wanted to support soldiers at East Orange General Hospital in New Jersey. They wore the iconic red-and-white striped uniforms, which, although aren't as abundant today, still act as a symbol of the cheerfulness and goodwill volunteering at a hospital can bring. Consider reaching out to your local hospital and asking if you could help out!

Candy stripers often need people to act as nurse's aids, clean up facilities, aid in patient cheer, or help draw up medicines. There are several opportunities if you reach out and get connected. Volunteering in healthcare settings is a great way to not only give back but also to learn more about the healthcare system and others in your community. In fact, there are loads of benefits that volunteering as a candy striper provides, such as enhanced empathy and compassion, improved leadership and teamwork skills, real-world healthcare exposure for aspiring medical professionals, and the opportunity to give back to the community

Key Takeaways:

In this chapter, we discussed ways to truly make yourself and others as healthy as possible. This is done by ensuring that you take care of yourself—and others—fully, including both mental and physical health. Beyond that, it also means ensuring the overall health of your community!

By forming a community group around shared interests, you are able to form connections and create a supportive network within your neighborhood with like-minded people. Whether it's cooking, gardening, painting, or any other hobby, starting a community group allows you to share your enthusiasm and strengthen bonds with people you might not have ever interacted with before. When starting a community group—or even just seeking one out—it's important to explore activities or hobbies you already enjoy doing with friends (or ones you have been really wanting to try) so that you can not only enjoy your time but also use that time to enhance your relationships and create lasting memories with others in your neighborhood. Whether it's learning a new skill, embarking on a creative project, engaging in a shared interest, participating in activities, or traveling somewhere new, pursuing new interests in community groups strengthens connections and promotes well-being—both mental and physical. Another great way to support your mental well-being is by honing your spirituality and growing closer to others in a group setting that allows for spiritual fellowship. This kind of community group can really hold you accountable and also deepen your connection, understanding, and relationship with the members of your group as you all share your spiritual journeys.

Next, we discussed community gardens and how they do more than just beautify neighborhoods, but also provide fresh produce, promote healthier lifestyles, and strengthen community bonds. By participating in community gardening projects, individuals can contribute to their community's collective physical and mental health. After all, who doesn't need a bit of nature in their life? Studies show that more exposure to the great outdoors and nature has a correlation to good health. In fact, we learned in this chapter that providing food for wildlife creates opportunities to observe nature, reduce stress, and promote biodiversity right in your back yard. Bird feeders, in particular, support bird populations and offer entertainment and relaxation for observers. Other ways nature (or the great outdoors) can benefit your health include:

- **Planting trees**: Planting trees benefits the environment, improves air quality, reduces energy costs, and enhances community aesthetics. By participating in tree-planting initiatives, individuals can contribute to a greener and healthier community while enjoying the many benefits that trees provide.

- **Through farmers' markets:** Similar to gardening in your community, shopping at farmers' markets also can greatly benefit your health as fresh produce is nutritionally dense and healthier for you. However, supporting these types of shops also strengthens the local economy and fosters connections between farmers and consumers.

By supporting local farmers and artisans, individuals contribute to the vitality of their community and enjoy unique and seasonal products.

- **From joining Parks and Recreation committees or events:** Getting involved in Parks and Recreation committees allows individuals to contribute to their community's well-being, support local initiatives, and promote outdoor recreation. Whether through volunteering, participating in events, or joining committees, individuals can play a role in enhancing their community's parks and recreational opportunities.

Being outside in nature is great—but there are additionally many more ways to support health in your community and these include:

- **Hosting exercise Sessions**: Building a gym community fosters connections, promotes physical fitness, and creates a supportive environment for achieving fitness goals. By organizing exercise sessions and events, individuals can engage with their community and work together toward healthier lifestyles.

- **Participating in community watch programs**: Community watch programs promote safety, reduce crime, and build stronger communities through collaboration and vigilance. By participating in or supporting community watch programs, individuals can contribute to a safer and more secure neighborhood for themselves and their neighbors.

- **Volunteering and supporting Anti-Drug Coalitions**: Supporting anti-drug coalitions helps raise awareness about substance abuse, provide resources for prevention and treatment, and empower communities to address drug-related issues. By volunteering or supporting anti-drug initiatives, individuals can contribute to a healthier and safer community for all.

- **Participate in Candy-Striping or Volunteer at a Nursing Home**: Volunteering in healthcare settings provides valuable support to patients, promotes empathy and compassion, and offers opportunities for personal growth and learning. Whether as a Candy Striper or a volunteer at a nursing home, individuals can make a meaningful difference in the lives of others while gaining valuable experience and skills.

Chapter 5

Support Your Neighborhood Businesses

It can be easy to overlook the significance of local businesses. However, they are truly community staples. Whether it's the corner bakery, the neighborhood bookstore, or the hardware store down the street, all local businesses play a vital role in shaping the character and vitality of our towns and cities. Unlike their corporate counterparts, local businesses offer a personal touch that can truly enrich our communities. In this chapter, we delve into the importance of supporting local businesses and also explore practical ways to cultivate a thriving economy at a local level. Whether you're a longtime advocate for small businesses or someone discovering the value of local commerce for the first time, this chapter invites you to harness it as another way to love your community.

Shop Local

If you want your community to continue to develop, it has to offer something that others don't. A great place to start is at the mom-and-pop places around town! No other town will have the same stores run by the same people if they're small businesses! Local business is a great way to stand out as a community—but, in order for that to happen, people have to show their support to these businesses. Because think about it—they can't exactly stay open if they're not selling anything or providing services! So, in order to do this, it's recommended that you shop local!

In fact, there is a major economic benefit of shopping locally that truly needs to be addressed and acted upon, no matter where your community is located. Local shopping is crucial to continued growth because the success of small, local businesses attracts and encourages other entrepreneurs to start local businesses. This leads to more jobs and revenue throughout the community. In fact, the statistical argument for shopping locally is super compelling. Studies show that for every one hundred dollars spent at a locally-owned business, more than seventy-three dollars remain in the community. Comparing that to a big-box store, only around forty-three dollars remain in the local economy. This shows a huge uptick in economic growth when you shop locally. But there are more benefits to consider as well, such as:

- **Keeping money local**: We just discussed the importance of this, but it still should be listed as a benefit. When you keep money local, you are funding your community and its vital services such as police and fire protection, street repairs, and trash collection.

- **Local decisions:** When you support a small business, you come to realize that the important decisions of the company are made by people who live in your community. They feel the impact of every decision that is made, as well!

- **Local products:** Local business owners often sell local products that are made by people they know or people they have a close business relationship with. This can mean better quality, and it also helps preserve the community feel and create more jobs/opportunities for everyone to benefit.

- **Discovering interesting people:** Getting to know the store owners is a great reason to shop local.

- **Product knowledge:** Local business owners are generally well-informed about the products they sell or the services they offer. They also know their customers and can adjust their inventories as needed to serve them.

- **Better service:** Most small business owners do what they do because they are passionate about their products or services. They also typically take more time to get to know their customers and go to further lengths to make them happy!

- **Support future growth:** As stated earlier, when you keep business local, you keep your money local and therefore create jobs to grow your community in the future.

Show up to Ribbon Cuttings and Events

Another great way to support your community and neighborhood businesses is by attending ribbon-cutting ceremonies. These are more than just symbolic events; they're powerful gatherings that signify the growth and prosperity of a community. Whether you're a business owner, a member of a chamber of commerce, or just a local and supportive resident, attending a ribbon-cutting event can offer a range of benefits. These include:

- **Supporting businesses:** Ribbon-cutting events provide an excellent opportunity to show your support for a business. By attending these ceremonies, you're demonstrating solidarity with businesses as a community member and letting them know you're there!

- **Network with key stakeholders:** Ribbon-cutting ceremonies attract a diverse array of attendees, including business owners, chamber members, local government officials, and community leaders. It's an ideal setting to expand your network (especially if you want to enhance your own visibility), forge important and valuable connections, and exchange ideas with potentially like-minded individuals with an interest in your community.

- **Discover new opportunities:** Whether you're in the market for new products or services or seeking potential collaboration on opportunities, ribbon-cutting events can offer a chance to discover them.

Enjoy Community Festivals

Attending fairs and festivals is another great way to show your love for your community. They are generally much more than just annual events filled with fun rides, cotton candy, and games. They are actually at times a vital thread in the fabric of your community. They often speak to people, cultures, and traditions that make your community unique.

Preserving Traditions and Heritage

Fairs and local community festivals can be a great place to see community traditions and heritage. They often showcase local crafts, music, food, and art, allowing residents to connect with their roots and even pass down cultural practices to future generations.

Economic Impact

Fairs and festivals are economic engines that drive traffic to local businesses that may not have otherwise had the exposure needed. It's also a great way for people who don't have storefronts to showcase their products!

Building Social Bonds

Festivals are a great way to get outside and enjoy the day. With a ton of food, shops, vendors, games, etc. in front of you, you can surely enjoy a special time with loved ones and neighbors. It's a great way to get everyone to interact and a wonderful way to form new bonds.

Education and Entertainment

Fairs and festivals can offer a unique blend of education and entertainment. They may feature agricultural exhibits, animal shows, or even interactive displays that educate people about elements of the community such as its local history. All the while, festivals and fairs can be home to some impeccable entertainment options such as concerts, car shows, amusement rides, and food festivals! There really is something for everyone.

Give Shout-Outs to Small Businesses Online

Following a business on social media can help more than you think. Word of mouth is how most small businesses thrive, and their social media presence generally is lacking. By liking them online, you may potentially give them more exposure. Consider leaving local businesses reviews, liking and sharing their posts, and telling friends and family to do the same.

Buy Small Business Gift Cards as Presents

Gift cards can be a strategic move to propel your small, local businesses forward. You can show support by buying them for others. In fact, gift cards make ideal presents for individuals of all ages. Gift cards help because they:

- **Offer flexibility:** Gift cards are great because they allow the recipient to choose their own present and use it when they want!

- **Offer the opportunity to try a new place:** This can bring new foot traffic into small establishments by incentivizing the person you're gifting to try something new!

Key Takeaways:

The truth of the matter is that supporting local businesses stimulates the economy by keeping money circulating within the community. As we explored, for every one hundred dollars spent at a local business, significantly more stays within the local economy compared to spending at non-local businesses. This results in more wealth staying in the community to stimulate the local economy, which can then lead to a higher standard of living.

In this chapter, we have also learned that shopping locally provides other benefits such as:

- **Unique offerings:** Shopping locally provides access to diverse products and services, often unavailable at national chain stores. Local businesses curate their offerings based on community preferences, offering a personalized shopping experience and promoting local artisans and farmers.

- **Personal connection:** Building relationships with local business owners fosters a sense of community and trust. These entrepreneurs are passionate about their products and take pride in providing exceptional customer service, going the extra mile to meet their customers' needs. They also are likely to shift inventory around to appease their consumers.

- **Long-term impact:** Supporting local businesses is an investment in the future of your community. By patronizing local businesses, you contribute to the prosperity and resilience of your neighborhoods. Local businesses also reinvest in their communities by supporting important services, such as police and fire protection, street maintenance, and waste management. They also contribute to local nonprofits and other businesses at a higher rate than larger corporations, which in turn strengthens the community even more.

By embracing local commerce and actively supporting neighborhood businesses, you play a crucial role in shaping the character, vitality, and future success of your own community! So, get out there and shop local!

Chapter 6

Get Together and Network

In today's fast-paced world, developing meaningful connections with those around us has never been more crucial. This chapter explores the significance of coming together as neighbors, colleagues, and friends to cultivate a sense of community and belonging—which is what this guide is all about!

From organizing block parties to sharing meals and participating in book clubs, the avenues for building relationships are abundant. Strangers can become friends through simple gestures like simply introducing themselves to our neighbors or offering assistance when it's needed. Laying the groundwork for genuine connections can truly enrich our lives and strengthen the social aspect of our communities, moving us closer and making us stronger.

Invite People Over for a Block Party

Neighborhoods often feel more secure once neighbors have become acquainted. Think about it—don't you feel better when you get to know your child's teacher? Their coach? Why wouldn't getting to know those in your community mean just as much to you? When we get to know one another, we can feel more at ease with who we're sharing space with.

Church leaders wanting to get to know their community might organize a block party. You could do the same! It can be a great way to meet the neighbors and develop friendships. A key goal of a block party, besides having fun, should be to build relationships. If you want to plan one, make sure you:

- **Have a clear goal:** Most block parties have a general purpose and that is to enjoy music, food, and conversation. Playing games and dancing are also great additions to this. They turn into wonderful ways to get to know others in the community. But, if you have a specific purpose, make sure that you pave that out beforehand so you're able to achieve it. For example, if you're hoping to get to know the adults first, think about having childcare areas so adults can mingle a little more freely.

- **Do some research:** Get in touch with the neighbors. Even before setting a time and date, talk one-on-one with people about if they'd be interested in coming. It doesn't hurt to network and put feelers out just to make sure it can be a success! This is also a great time to ask what people like to eat or what kind of music they enjoy!

- **Invite everyone:** In some neighborhoods, it may be possible to go door-to-door with flyers. If it isn't, though, don't forget about social media! Social media messages can often spread quickly and be more efficient than flyers when you're hoping for a large turnout and wanting to cover large ground. But whatever you do—make sure you extend the invite to everyone in your community! Let people feel like they belong! That's what you want to do by reaching out, so make sure everyone is included.

- **Offer food:** Food is a central part of a block party's success. If you want more people to come, offer food! A potluck is also a great, inexpensive way to get people interested in participating. It is also a great way to try new foods! You can even consider having people sign up for what they're bringing. Although, with a lot of attendees, this might be difficult to manage. If you're interested in providing the entire meal, don't be afraid to ask around for donations! Local farms and restaurants might be willing to donate to the event (especially if it's a large one) in exchange for advertisement!

- **Add music and games:** Besides food, music and games are key ingredients to a successful party. Make sure you have something that everyone can enjoy—and have a little of everything. Consider picnic games like bean bag tosses (cornhole), relay or sack races, fair games, or even scavenger hunts! Add music, both live (ask around in your neighborhood to see who might do it for free) and recorded, to the mix, and be sure to provide a quality sound system.

- **Obey the law:** Above all else, make sure you're following the rules. The last thing you want to do is go down as the person who threw the party that got everyone a ticket (or worse, arrested). Many municipalities require a permit if your block party will close down a street, redirect traffic, or be located in a public park. Keep in mind that if a public site is used, it will need to be cleaned up afterward. Make sure you pay attention to all local ordinances.

Cook a Meal for a Neighbor

Have you ever had a bad day and come home to a good home-cooked meal? Whether provided by a parent, a grandparent, aunt, uncle, or even a friend or significant other—you have likely experienced this at least once. Didn't it make you feel better? Providing a home-cooked meal for someone going through a challenging or stressful time is a simple way to bring support and comfort right to their doorstep. When a series of friends, family, and colleagues join a Meal Train it not only multiplies the meals, but it also really shows love and care for someone! In times when someone you care for is experiencing distress, a meal can really help!

However, if someone in your community has suffered a loss, maybe opt to skip a home-cooked meal in this scenario and instead gift them with a food gift card. When people experience a loss, they often experience an influx of meals from people wishing to help out. So a gift card ensures they are not overwhelmed and can be flexible with your offering.

However, other times, a home-cooked meal is much-needed. If you know your neighbor is struggling in a relationship, has lost their job, or is going through any particularly difficult situation (divorce, custody battle, medical issue, friendship disaster, or any other situation where they may just be a little down on themselves), consider fixing dinner for them so they don't have to worry about doing it for themselves and can instead focus on healing!

Start a Book Club

The benefits of a book club may not be so obvious to you outside of just reading a lot of books. Sure, the primary benefit is the opportunity to read a book and discuss it with others. But there are a lot of benefits that make the experience worth it!

So, whether you are thinking of starting a new book club or joining a book club—or are questioning whether the current group you're in is right for you—consider the following benefits and get a little insight:

- **Book clubs get you outside of your normal comfort zone:** We all have that genre or two we gravitate toward. Being in a book club opens the doors to various other genres that we may not have thought of or considered before! This can help broaden horizons. And you never know—your new favorite book might turn out to be one you would have never read had you not been in the club!

- **They keep you accountable for reading:** The average American reads just a handful of books per year. Even when you factor in avid readers, the average only climbs to around twelve per year (one per month). With work, family, streaming services, chores, etc., it's easy to miss out on reading time. However, by committing to a book club, you are committing to reading books. While there may be times you don't finish the book, and may not even start it, keeping the commitment to your group will be a priority more times than it isn't, which will result in you reading more.

- **Encourages you to read more thoughtfully:** Not only will you read more books, but you will also read them more thoughtfully. A book club is all about discussing the book (often with the bonus of tasty snacks, too). Rather than skipping or skimming certain areas of the book, you're more likely to really focus on having something to talk about. Discovering a book's nuances is one of the best parts of discussion time. And actively searching for themes, exploring interesting characters, and forming a true opinion of the work will keep words in your mouth during the meeting!

- **Promotes social engagement:** Likely the most important aspect, as far as this guide is concerned. It really is all about getting together with others in the community, having some wine, eating snacks, and catching up. Of course, discussing books is a great aspect and keeps everyone even more interested, but it's really about growing a bond with people in your area!

Introduce Yourself to Neighbors

Sometimes just simply introducing yourself is the biggest and most important gesture. Whether you're just moving to the neighborhood, someone else is moving in, or you've been there for a long time but haven't made the full rounds yet, it is quite important to introduce yourself to your neighbors!

Of course, moving to a new home can be a really daunting process. You have to pack all your stuff, move it (which can get grueling), and unpack everything! It might seem like you have a lot more important things on your to-do list than meeting the neighbors. This can lead to not knowing them, even after years of living right next to them. And this happens to the best of us—even those who consider themselves extroverted!

So, whether you're brand new to the area, or just haven't gotten around to meeting your neighbors, make sure you try to make an impression somehow!

Say "Hello"

Saying "hello" can be easy, but it can also be difficult! If you see your neighbor out in the yard, a simple wave can be a great and friendly way to acknowledge them. However, it usually takes more than that to really get to know someone. You can send a nice card or a letter to say hello to them, especially if you're busy (or they are). It's perfectly okay to not want to interrupt them or to have a fear of rejection. Sometimes writing a letter or a note is a great option. You can stick it under their door or even in their mailbox and in just a few sentences let them know a little something about you!

You can also try icebreakers if you would prefer to introduce yourself in person (or you can choose to do these if you want to leave a note, too). Consider adding a few freshly cut flowers or maybe some homemade cookies! These will definitely make a great first impression!

Ask Questions and Consider Asking for Help

If you've moved into a new area, it would only make sense that you would have a lot of questions. Those questions make great conversation starters. "Where can they find the best deals on meat?", "What day is the farmer's market?", "Where are these places located?", Instead of searching on Google, simply ask your neighbors for their input! Once you get the answers you're looking for, you can start chatting with them about other things and use that to identify a few common interests!

It's not just about asking questions, though! You could even strike up a conversation about needing some help moving your furniture or carrying a heavy item up the stairs. While most people may feel a bit uneasy asking for help from a complete stranger, most people would be more than happy to help with something quickly. Even if you don't need help moving in, consider asking for help for something else. Maybe you need to borrow a power tool or a ladder—or maybe you need help installing something. You can even offer to pay them for their help!

Observe

This doesn't mean to start stalking your neighbors or being nosey. There is a healthy dose of observation that can be done without being weird or creepy. It's all about paying attention to identify common interests you may have. For example, if you notice your neighbors grilling up ribs, and you also have a love for grilling, that's a great in! You may ask if they want to do a barbeque with you. Or, if your neighbor walks into their house with a set of golf clubs, chances are he might be playing a round or two every so often! If you're a fan of golf, just ask for more details or even invite them to play with you sometime!

Offer Help

Just as you may ask for help from time to time, make sure you know there are many ways you could offer help to your neighbors, too. If they ask you to borrow something that you have, don't hesitate to give it to them. This would be a great way to show them that you trust them, and it could signify the beginning of a great friendship.

There are also ways you can actively offer help without them asking for it, too. For example, if your neighbor is older and carrying something heavy, offer to help them carry it! Little acts of kindness can really go a long way in helping you get to meet everyone in the area and find out more about them and their daily lives.

Walk Around

That's right! Just walking around is sometimes exactly what you need to do to get to know the goings on in the neighborhood and to introduce yourself more appropriately. Besides, spending time outside will give you the opportunity to get some fresh air as well. While you're soaking in the sun and walking around the block, say "hi" to those people you pass or see along the way. Making sure to spend time outside during the weekend and after work can give you the best opportunity to meet others. After all, that's when most people go out to do their shopping or leisure activities.

If you have a garden or a front porch, use it to your benefit, too! Not only can you get your chores done, or just enjoy some nature, you might be surprised to see just how many people talk to you.

Be Friendly and Make a Real Effort

Whatever approach you decide to follow to meet your neighbors, just make sure you're friendly, and that you're yourself! People will appreciate the extra effort you are putting into making new friends and they will likely return the favor. By being nice, kind, and polite you will show your neighbors that you're positive and can be a great friend. Keep in mind that touching upon topics such as TV shows, music, or just your favorite recipes is a great way to keep a conversation rolling with someone you don't know very well.

Don't Be Pushy

You should definitely be talkative, friendly, and polite when approaching one of your neighbors. However, keep in mind not to be too pushy and aim to keep it short and sweet. No one wants to feel like they're being interrogated. Your very first conversations/interactions with your neighbors should be slightly generic, and they shouldn't be very lengthy. Ask them about the neighborhood, the town, and where everything is, and leave it at that. Leave it up to them to continue chatting or invite you to do something. Don't expect much during your first interaction. Most people won't jump right into inviting you to do things (although this does happen from time to time), so be patient. It will definitely pay off in the long run, and you'll slowly start bonding with your neighbors. Treat it like a plant...water it and tend to it and eventually there will be something big and beautiful.

Host a Gathering

This is one of the most fun ways to get to know your neighbors. If you have just moved in, though, this can be a little more difficult. Of course, there's a ton of stuff to unpack, and, after all that work, the last thing you may want to do is host a gathering or plan a big event. However, it doesn't have to be planned to the T, and it's possible that if you're reading this guide, you aren't new and just need a little extra push to get to know your neighbors on a deeper level.

Regardless of your situation, it's important to note that people generally understand other people. If you did just move in, people will be aware of that. They wouldn't expect you to host a multi-course dinner party with the finest China, cutlery, and linens. Likewise, you wouldn't expect that of someone else who was new to the area.

Most people are just fine with a casual get-together. In fact, this makes a majority of people more comfortable. You can even make it a BYOS (Bring Your Own Snack) event and do it outside! People like hanging out outside, and BYOS events are great, icebreaking sort of evenings that can get rid of all the awkwardness that can accompany hanging out for the first time!

Be Authentic, Be Yourself

Remember, there's no point in pretending to be someone you're not just to please the neighbors or force them to like you. What would be the point in developing a relationship with someone and being accepted for something that you aren't? Of course, the first impression counts, and it's always advised to be the best version of yourself in the beginning. However, that doesn't mean being someone completely different. Although first impressions are important, they do fade as relationships develop. You want to be honest with others. If you aren't, you'll be cheating yourself and them out of a friendship.

Do Something for Someone in Need

There is evidence to suggest that when people help other people, they promote certain physiological changes in the brain that are also linked with happiness. There could be many reasons for this, including being more physically active as a result of volunteering. Or it could also be because volunteering makes us more socially active. Whatever the case, helping others can help us be healthier. But most importantly, it can help us make new friends and connect with our community on a much deeper level. Face-to-face activities such as volunteering at a homeless shelter or hospital can also help reduce loneliness and isolation, which is what this chapter is all about—getting together and networking.

Studies show that volunteering enhances an individual's overall sense of purpose and identity. This is because helping others (and just being around others) can make you feel rewarded, fulfilled, and empowered. Helping others, especially those who are less fortunate than yourself, can really help put things into perspective and make you feel more positive about your own circumstances, no matter what struggles you may be facing. Helping people in need and volunteering have been linked to various benefits including:

- **Monkey-see, monkey-do:** Studies have found that people are more likely to perform acts of generosity after observing someone else do the same. This becomes a bit of a ripple effect throughout the community with several people vying to make a difference!

- **Destressing:** Research shows that regular volunteering can improve your ability to manage stress and stave off disease. It can also increase your overall satisfaction with life, which makes sense since it has been linked to making individuals feel less lonely!

- **Greater self-esteem:** People who volunteer have been found to have higher self-esteem. Volunteering makes you feel good about yourself! Note: the benefits of volunteering can also depend on your consistency. This means the more often you volunteer, the greater your self-esteem!

- **More positivity:** When you help others, you give off a positive aura that can be infectious! Don't forget that being a force for good can really help people create a lasting bond with you. Having positive impacts on others' lives can really help the world become a better place. Plus, it can even help change your own outlook and attitude within yourself. Experts say that performing acts of kindness can really boost your own mood, which in turn makes you a generally more optimistic and positive person.

Key Takeaways:

This chapter is all about the act of coming together with others, whether that be through block parties, shared meals, or clubs. Getting together with others and socializing is fundamental to building strong and vibrant communities as it provides opportunities to connect, share experiences, and foster a sense of belonging with one another.

Simple acts of kindness, such as introducing yourself to neighbors or offering assistance to them, can truly have a huge impact on a community and the people who reside in it, individually. These gestures lay the foundation for meaningful relationships and contribute to a culture of compassion and support—which, at the end of the day, is what we all want in a community! Be your most authentic self, learn from others, and lift others up! You will gain more positivity by helping others and by breathing that kindness into your life, and, consequently, others will gravitate toward you!

Chapter 7

Celebrate Kindness

Kindness is everything when learning to love your community. Kindness is the gentle gesture from a stranger, the helping hand extended in times of need, and the genuine warmth shared between neighbors. It's in the very foundation of being a community—and this chapter is all about celebrating it!

From the simple act of offering a smile to someone passing you in the street to the generosity of volunteering our time and skills, kindness doesn't really know any bounds. No amount of kindness is too little or too big. It transcends barriers of language and culture and can really pull us into a shared humanity. Everyone recognizes kindness!

In this chapter, we delve into the ways in which we can spread kindness within our neighborhoods, schools, and beyond. Remember, as we explore the art of giving and the power of empathy, we have the ability to touch the lives of others and truly transform our communities little by little for the better.

Put Together Small Holiday/Seasonal Gifts for Neighbors

The golden rule to life is to treat others the way you want to be treated, and this includes your neighbors. The truth is that you may not see your neighbors very often, but that doesn't matter! They live next to you and are part of the community that you want to learn to love just a little more than you did yesterday. Start with your neighbors and branch out from there. Remember them, just as you do everyone else, during the holidays or other celebrations! It can truly make them feel special to receive a gift, no matter how small. Consider making small gift bags for them, taking them a tin of cookies, or sending out holiday cards—just a small token to show you care!

Offer Your Skillset for Free

We all spend so much time on our work that it's hard to imagine giving away some of those valuable hours for free. But there are lots of benefits to be had from donating your professional skills.

When you volunteer your professional time and skills, you are not only helping others, but you are also helping yourself, as there are still some self-serving benefits that come with it. You expand your network, raise your profile, and build relationships that could eventually lead to paying jobs in the future!

But the core of this act is to express your expertise without worrying about revenue or what it can do for you. This is all about ways to be kind and spread kindness throughout your community. And the truth of the matter is, you won't have to look far to find places seeking volunteers or skill sets for free! It doesn't matter whether you have organizing and administrative skills, handyman skills, accounting prowess, marketing genius, or any other skill set—it can be used! Anywhere and everywhere! But some places you can begin to start offering your services include schools and other programs, local groups or a chamber of commerce, hospitals or nursing homes, and senior living facilities. And, of course, you can offer your services directly to your neighbors.

Helping at any of these places will have a positive impact on the community, and your skillset can generally always be used by someone for something. By giving your time and skills for free, you are sharing yourself and your expertise in a way that allows you to feel connected on a personal and professional level.

Help Your Neighbors with Chores

One of the best things about being in a great community is the sense of connection and belonging that can come along with it. Being kind to those who live near you is what this chapter is all about. We are truly homing in on the ideology of "treat others the way you wish to be treated".

Some great ways to show your neighbors kindness are listed below:

- **Help with yard work:** If you notice your neighbor is struggling to keep up with their lawn or garden, try and step up and lend a hand. You never know what someone is dealing with that could prevent them from being able to handle their lawn! We all get busy, but you never know if someone is having trouble physically, struggling with depression, or if they're just stressed and busy with everyday life. Helping them out could be exactly what they need!

- **Invite them over for food:** Planning a dinner party or cookout is a great way to bring people together. Extend an invitation to a few of your neighbors, as well as their families, to come over for some good food and fun!

- **Run errands for them:** Sometimes life gets hectic for everyone. By picking up groceries or dropping off a package at the post office for someone, you can really be a huge help and make a giant difference. This is especially true for someone who is elderly or has restricted mobility.

- **Bring them treats:** If you're baking something one day, why not make a few extra and take some over to your neighbors? You might want to take potential dietary restrictions into consideration if you know someone has an allergy or illness, but baking some cookies or muffins and dropping them off can really mean a lot to someone!

- **Assist with childcare:** Childcare is expensive, and sometimes it's not always easy to find. If there are some young children in your neighborhood, offer to watch them for a few hours to give the parents a much-needed break. If you have kids of your own, consider making it a play date. And you never know—maybe your neighbors will return the favor someday!

- **Share your garden goods:** Nothing beats fresh produce. If you end up with a larger yield than you were expecting, hand off those fruits and veggies to other people on the block! This could really make someone's day since not only are you offering high-quality food, but you're also helping them save on their groceries this week!

- **Take their pet(s) for a walk:** If you're an animal lover, there really isn't a better way to get some exercise. Walking a neighbor's pet is a great way to help them and yourself. These days, some people walk their cats as well as their dogs, so don't forget the felines! You could offer to walk them, too!

- **Help with household repairs:** If you're handy around the house, consider being that way at your neighbor's place, too! Every homeowner will tell you there's always something to repair, maintain, or upgrade around the house, and you never know when someone's list is overwhelming! Offer to help out! There should be plenty of opportunities.

Fundraise for Schools

Unequal, insufficient funding for schools in the United States has long driven the need for fundraising efforts to supplement school budgets. But unless you work in the education sector, are a PTA/PTO leader or volunteer, or are a seasoned parent who knows the inner workings, you may not know that the importance of fundraising can go well beyond supplementing the budget.

When school staff, volunteers, and students all come together to work toward a common goal, the entire community is strengthened.

Adults and children can bond, learn new and exciting things, and use their experiences to enrich their lives inside and outside of school. By getting involved in raising money for the school system in your community, you are not only providing a much-needed resource (money) but you are also becoming a resource. You are becoming a piece of the school community—someone who cares about the education and future of young people. Helping the school raise money is important because it:

- **Enriches our children's educations:** It might seem obvious, but the amount of money a school has is tied directly to the value of education for the youth in that school. Research clearly indicates that lower school funding correlates to lower education outcomes. This includes lower achievement scores and graduation rates, which also translates to fewer post-secondary opportunities for students in poorly funded schools. This is an issue that needs to be rectified, and fundraising helps close the gap. Efforts go beyond students' basic academic necessities such as classroom materials, updated technology, and clean, safe facilities. It also encompasses what goes on outside the classroom as well, such as extracurricular enrichment programs in the arts and gifted and STEM programs. School fundraising helps bring these opportunities to a wider range of students and allows for a more well-rounded education for all on a more equal playing field.

- **Helps children learn important life skills:** While there is a wide range of fundraisers that can be effective, those that involve student participation can have a unique result.

Teaching children how to raise money for something important teaches them important life skills and values. This is because it forces them to set goals, plan, be accountable, work as a team, learn what it means to lead, etc. Plus, having a direct stake in their own school's well-being can really teach them the importance of putting effort into making their world a better place.

- **Strengthens school-community bonds:** Research shows that students do better when schools and communities communicate and work together to create a better environment for the students. This is for a few reasons. First, the more community involvement there is in a school, the more funds they typically have to work with. Therefore, students have access to more resources. But it also allows for students, staff, parents, and community members to spend time together and learn more about each other's needs, which creates more opportunities for improvement inside the school.

Create and Maintain Traditions with Neighbors

One of the most beautiful things about living in a community is the relationships that can be formed in them. Neighbors can truly become more than just people who live next to you, or on the same street. They can become friends, confidants, and even as close as family. This can happen naturally over time or be intentional. Regardless, it's important to note that creating and maintaining traditions with neighbors can be just as fun and meaningful as creating and maintaining traditions with your family members!

One of the for neighbors to become like family is through shared experiences. Whether it's a block party, a neighborhood cleanup, or even just a casual conversation over the fence, these experiences can create a sense of camaraderie and belonging. There's a shift that happens once we become familiar with others. This is no different for our neighbors, who are able to become closer and more familiar the more time we spend with them. And the more time we spend with them, the greater opportunity we have to share experiences that can lead to a true relationship. When neighbors come together to work toward a common goal, they begin to see each other as more than just people who happen to live on the same street. They become a team, and that team mentality can quickly turn neighbors into family.

There are many ways that you can develop traditions with your neighbors. And these traditions can take many forms, such as:

- **Block parties:** As we touched on previously in this guide, block parties are a classic neighborhood tradition that has been around for decades. If your community already has the tradition of block parties, make sure you uphold them. If they don't already have them in place, consider creating one. They are a great way to get to know your neighbors and build relationships with those who live around you. They can be organized for any occasion, from a barbeque celebrating the start of summer to a Halloween costume party/trick-or-treat event. They can be as simple or as elaborate as you want! The biggest key is to make sure that everyone feels welcome and included. To make the most of block party events, consider organizing games and activities for kids and adults alike and encouraging everyone to bring a dish to share. Games, various dishes, and a heaping pile of fun are sure to create multitudes of conversations and create great connections between neighbors.

- **Holiday celebrations:** Holiday celebrations can be a great way to bring neighbors together and celebrate the season. Whether it's a Christmas party, a Hanukkah celebration, or a Fourth of July cookout, holiday events can help to create a sense of community and become wonderful traditions to uphold. To make holiday traditions with neighbors and community members a success, consider organizing activities that everyone can participate in, young and old! This can be something like a cookie decorating contest or a competition where you carve pumpkins! Don't forget the food, too! Who doesn't want food around the holidays? Consider a potluck for a fun tradition where everyone can get a taste for something new as well!

- **Volunteer events:** Maybe during certain times of the year, or once a quarter, you and your neighbors get together for a common cause! Volunteer events are another great way to bring neighbors together and make a positive impact in the community. Whether it's a neighborhood clean-up or a food drive, these events can really create a sense of purpose and result in everyone working together as a team for the common good! This is a great tradition because it not only brings everyone together but also helps others!

Participate in (or Start) Decorating Events

Decorating events are a great opportunity to get involved with your community and have a little fun. It's also a great way to really let your kindness wings spread by letting loose and enjoying one another's home-front decorating abilities! Be social, be supportive, be encouraging! Have fun and let loose! These events can be mixed into holiday celebrations but can also happen all year round.

Many neighborhoods choose a different festive theme every year. Holding a voting session in the community is the best way to determine what this theme will be as it adds a bit of democracy to the process!

Consider adding a prize at the end of the year, or a list of prizes to be awarded in which everyone votes. Remember, the idea for these is to also be cohesive with one another, so working as a team is encouraged. Other people will be seeing your neighborhood decorated in all its glory. The more you work together, the more impressive the overall aesthetic will be!

Christmas trees are an example that can and festive cheer! Set up a Christmas tree in an accessible space and decorate it using the theme you all have voted on! You can even make a fun, annual tradition out of a tree-lighting ceremony, where you all light your outdoor trees at the same time! Get some hot drinks together, put on some Christmas music, and just enjoy the night! You can also take it a step further and add a ton of Christmas lights! Because who doesn't love Christmas lights? Illuminate your neighborhood with as many strings of light as you can with the theme you all chose! The sky is the limit!

Refrain from Gossiping

When trying to build a stronger community, one of the most crucial practices is to refrain from engaging in gossip. Gossip is defined as idle talk or rumors about the personal or private affairs of others, and all it does is erode trust, breed negativity, and create divisions within a community. Steer clear of it yourself and avoid others who gossip.

By consciously choosing to abstain from gossip, you can contribute to the creation of a more positive and cohesive social environment. As the title suggests, you are looking for ways to love your community, not gossip about them and breed negativity.

Refraining from gossip truly demonstrates a respect for others' privacy, dignity, and emotional well-being. Every person deserves to be treated with kindness, empathy, and integrity, regardless of their background or circumstances. Engaging in gossip violates these principles by spreading potentially harmful or unfounded information about people, and is generally done without a person's consent or even their knowledge. By not participating in that harmful behavior, you will uphold a standard of ethical conduct and show others that you can be trusted. Being your authentic self and steering away from all of that negativity, makes others want to be their authentic self without fear of being judged or ridiculed. Rumors or hearsay truly signal dishonesty and steering away from them shows that you have integrity, and most people are more willing to invest in someone who has integrity.

They are also likely going to be willing to invest their time and care into building up a community that shows signs of integrity. Doing this allows for the environment you all reside in to feel safe so that others can share their thoughts, feelings, and experiences openly, knowing that they will be met with compassion and support.

When someone begins to show signs of gossiping about others in your community, simply tell them you are uncomfortable with the conversation and create a boundary (which we discussed earlier in the guide). If they don't respect that boundary, consider separating yourself from them in the future.

Advocate for Positive Change

Creating a vibrant and inclusive community requires more than just sporadic acts of kindness; it demands proactive leadership, persistent advocacy, and collective action to truly work. While small, and individual gestures of goodwill can inspire hope and connection (and every gesture is welcome, no matter how small), it is important to note that sustainable change requires a little more.

Leading by example is paramount in driving true community change. Rather than passively waiting for improvement, you must be ready to actively embody the values you wish to see in your community. If you're on the shyer side, this may be more difficult in some facets—but you can always be kind, and you can always be compassionate. Any time something requires a little more than you feel you're equipped to do (like being a voice to others if you're introverted and shy), consider leaning on a trusted friend, neighbor, significant other, etc. to help. Whether it's volunteering at local shelters, participating in neighborhood cleanups, or advocating for social justice causes, leading by example sets a precedent for others to follow and encourages widespread participation in building a better community. Remember "monkey-see, monkey-do"! Others are more apt to participate if they see someone else doing it first!

By being the change you want to see in your community, you are taking ownership of the issues within the community and working diligently to address them. Doing this requires courage and determination, as well as a ton of resilience in order to confront challenges and advocate for solutions. Whether it involves advocating for equitable access to education, promoting environmental sustainability, demanding change in local politics that threatens to disrupt your community, or championing greater diversity and inclusion, you must be willing to speak out, take action, and hold yourself and others accountable for creating positive change. This may take practice, patience, and a little grit—but, with the help of your community, you can do it.

Connect Deeply with Others

Establishing meaningful connections with others goes beyond surface-level interactions. It's all about trust, empathy, and understanding those around you, whether this be in your personal or professional life. But how do you move past casual conversations and create genuine relationships?

Be Curious

Genuine interest in others can be a powerful bonding tool. People can read when you're truly interested in them and curious about what it is that makes them unique. Ask open-ended questions that encourage them to share their thoughts, experiences, and aspirations. Listen attentively (use the active listening skills discussed in Chapter 2), without judgment, and respond thoughtfully to demonstrate your engagement.

Be Vulnerable

Being vulnerable isn't easy. We can all agree with that. And it's likely that being vulnerable is the last thing you want to do with someone you just met. However, it is critical to form deep and meaningful connections. Share your own stories, fears, dreams, and all the emotions in between to create a space for openness and trust. However, be mindful of boundaries—theirs and yours—and avoid oversharing, especially in the early stages of interaction. Don't be afraid to trust people, but it is a balancing act. You don't want to misplace your trust.

Be Empathetic

Empathy allows you to understand and connect with others on an emotional level. It's the opportunity to truly put yourself in someone else's shoes, acknowledge their feelings, and offer support without judgment. Avoid giving unsolicited advice and focus on validating their experiences. By being empathetic, you deepen your relationships and ensure that your friends and loved ones feel validated and understood.

Be Respectful

Respect forms the basis of all healthy relationships. Treat others with kindness, courtesy, dignity, and respect, and always honor their boundaries, limitations, and preferences. By doing these things, people will see you in a positive light. Maintain positive communication and avoid behaviors like gossiping or mocking and

you will show your integrity and character to others. This forms
the foundation of all deep connections—trust.

Be Generous

Generosity shows goodwill and appreciation in a relationship.
By offering your time, resources, or support to help others you
can help them achieve their goals and overcome challenges,
which opens the door to love and admiration. Celebrate others'
achievements, express gratitude for their contributions, and
help them as often as you can. Remember though, relationships
are two-way streets. Never allow your generosity to be taken
for granted. Don't be generous in hopes of a return—but don't
become a doormat, either.

Be Consistent

Consistency is key to building trust and reliability in your
community. Follow through on your commitments, check in
regularly with people, and show consistent support in both good
and bad times, and you will certainly be able to cultivate a deeper
connection with whomever you wish!

Spread Neighborhood Love/Positivity on Social Media

Social media plays a significant role in today's digital age. It
offers an unprecedented amount of opportunity to connect with
others, share stories, and celebrate what our communities and
neighborhoods have to offer. Leveraging the power of social media

to grow your influence in the community, breathe positivity, inspire change, and spread a little love, can be beneficial.

One of the simplest ways to spread love for your neighborhood via social media is by creating a Facebook, TikTok, Instagram, etc. for your community and sharing uplifting stories that highlight the positive aspects of life locally. Whether it's showcasing local businesses, spotlighting community events, or celebrating the accomplishments of neighbors, sharing positive content can inspire pride and unity among everyone in the community.

Use social media to thank volunteers, update people on local events, discuss local issues, share ideas for improvements (and collect feedback from others), mobilize support for community causes, discuss initiatives, etc.

Ultimately, by harnessing the power of social media, individuals can spread love for their neighborhood and develop and share a sense of community pride. So, get out there and share some social media love for your community!

Be Pleasant in Public

In our daily interactions, whether it's while we run errands, commute to work, or simply take a stroll in the neighborhood, the way we engage with others can have a profound impact on the atmosphere of our community. It can affect the way people see you and the place you live. Being pleasant in public not only contributes to more enjoyable interactions for you specifically, but it also cultivates a sense of kindness and goodwill among neighbors.

One of the simplest yet most powerful ways to be pleasant in public is by merely offering a smile and a friendly greeting whenever the situation arises. A warm smile and a simple "hello" can brighten someone's day and create a sense of connection and warmth, even among strangers. Remember, you never know what someone is going through! By acknowledging others with kindness, we can truly contribute to a culture of positivity and mutual respect.

Whether it's waiting in line at the grocery store, navigating crowded sidewalks, or dealing with traffic congestion, maintaining a calm and composed demeanor can help diffuse tensions and prevent conflicts from arising. It's normal to feel frustrated in these situations, but by exercising empathy and compassion toward others, we can really lead by example and create an atmosphere of mutual understanding and support, which is what we all want in our communities. Furthermore, showing appreciation and gratitude to everyone, especially service workers and frontline workers, can make a significant difference in everyone's day-to-day experiences.

You never know when someone is watching. This could be your reputation! By being pleasant in general and not allowing negativity to take hold, we can really foster the culture of kindness and respect that we all dream about existing in the world. Being pleasant in public also ensures we are good role models for young people in our communities.

Key Takeaways:

This chapter is all about celebrating kindness. While this guide is all about being a good neighbor and being kind, this chapter truly focuses on building community connections. After all, kindness serves as the cornerstone of community and can allow us to develop and grow bonds that transcend mere acquaintanceship. By extending acts of kindness to our neighbors, we not only strengthen the fabric of our communities but also cultivate a sense of belonging, which as we discussed at the beginning of this guide, is what life is all about!

By embracing empathy, we can truly walk in someone else's shoes. We can understand their joys, aspirations, and even their struggles. Through acts of compassion and understanding, we can cultivate a culture of inclusivity and support and build bridges that connect us. Who doesn't want to live in a neighborhood that truly consists of people just ready to serve and support one another?

And these communities don't just form overnight. They take connection. They take relationship. They also take model behavior. Whether it's offering our time, skills, or resources, generosity should know no bounds in a community. By embracing a spirit of generosity, we can truly create a ripple effect of positivity that touches lives and inspires others to pay it forward.

Another great way to build a deeper connection and harness kindness is by building and maintaining traditions within our neighborhoods. Traditions can help foster a sense of continuity and belonging. From block parties to celebrating the holidays with one another, these traditions strengthen community bonds and create cherished memories for generations to come.

Remember that kindness extends beyond individual actions. Kindness is the collective efforts that work toward positive change. By being consistent and advocating for a stronger community and more inclusivity, you can create a brighter, more compassionate future.

Chapter 8
Final Thoughts

As we conclude this journey of exploring ways to give back to our communities and foster stronger connections with those around us, let's take a moment to reflect on the impact of our collective efforts. Throughout this guide, we've delved into various strategies and actions that can make a meaningful difference in the lives of others and contribute to the overall well-being of our neighborhoods.

First and foremost, it's important to recognize the power of small acts of kindness. Whether it's lending a helping hand to a neighbor in need, supporting local businesses, or simply spreading positivity in our interactions with others, every gesture, no matter how small, has the potential to create ripple effects of goodwill within our communities.

Moreover, by coming together and collaborating with our neighbors, we have the opportunity to develop a sense of unity and solidarity that transcends individual differences and creates a shared sense of belonging. Through initiatives such as community events, neighborhood networks, and getting involved in local politics (and advocating for change where necessary), we can work together to address common challenges, celebrate diversity, and build a stronger, more inclusive community for all.

As we move forward, let's continue to embrace the spirit of generosity, empathy, and cooperation that lies at the heart of building vibrant, thriving communities. Let's remain open to new ideas, be willing to lend a helping hand, and be committed to making a positive impact, however small it may seem.

In closing, I encourage each and every one of you to keep dreaming, keep innovating, and keep striving to make your community a more beautiful, peaceful, and compassionate place for all who call it home. Together, you and your neighbors have the power to create a brighter, more hopeful future for generations to come. Thank you for taking this journey and learning the fifty ways to love your community. May your efforts inspire positive change in the world around us.